The Process of Writing

Discovery & Control

SECOND EDITION

VAN NOSTRAND   KNOBLAUCH   PETTIGREW

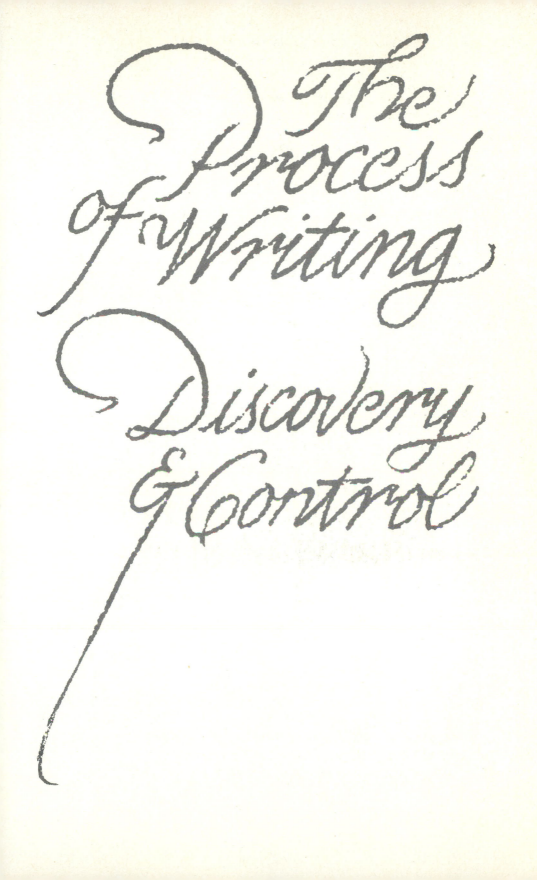

The Process of Writing

Discovery & Control

HOUGHTON MIFFLIN COMPANY   BOSTON

Dallas   Geneva, Illinois   Hopewell, New Jersey   Palo Alto   London

The Process of Writing

Discovery & Control

SECOND EDITION

A. D. Van Nostrand *Brown University*

C. H. Knoblauch *New York University*

Joan Pettigrew *Boston University*

Cover calligraphy by Jean Evans

Library of Congress Catalog Card Number: 81-83449

ISBN: 0-395-31755-X

Contents

3. The Writer's Purpose   31

4. The Nature of Evidence   41

Review of Part 1   51

Part 2: Writing to Readers   59

5. The Reader's Frame of Reference   60

6. Writing to Your Intended Reader   70

7. Evidence for the Reader   81

Review of Part 2   89

Part 3: Developing an Extended Statement   99

8. Forecasting a Written Statement   100

9. The Nature of an Extended Statement   111

10. The Diminishing Sequence   122

11. The Controlled Expanding Sequence   133

Review of Part 3   145

Preface

The purpose of this book is to make manageable the teaching and learning of the writing process. The act of writing—of making and expressing relationships—is enormously complex since it imposes so many different and simultaneous constraints on the writer. Instructors who have taught writing already know that the learner is engaged in a bewildering number of tasks and that, to guide a student in the writing process, one must be responsive to what that student is confronting.

To make the teaching and learning of the writing process more manageable, we have set three objectives for this book. One is to sort out the writing tasks in a way that enables the learner to become aware of them. Another is to support the instructor in engaging the learner in these tasks. The third is to provide a common vocabulary that enables the instructor and learner to talk about the writing process with precision and clarity. We have designed this book to simplify and demystify the process of writing and to avoid the simplistic and the superficial.

The book focuses on *process*, specifically on the choices that confront students as they write. Descriptive rather than prescriptive, the text illustrates the kinds of decisions a writer necessarily makes, without telling the writer what to decide. It explains strategies for discovery that the writer can use to generate information and to express new relationships, and it demonstrates strategies of control that the writer can mobilize to communicate these relationships clearly to a reader. But the book does not impose dogma. In short, it discusses the writer's options in a way that enables the instructor to select and emphasize those options that match the distinct needs of individual students. As they proceed, students can progressively take on responsibility for using strategies of composing to improve their communication and for analyzing models of professional writing and adapting these models to their own purposes.

This book has evolved from basic research in composition. Under the auspices of the Center for Research in Writing, the manuscript has evolved through four successive stages since its inception in 1973. The first published edition, entitled *Functional Writing* (1978), emphasized the dynamic and recursive nature of the writing process. This second edition, while retaining that focus, offers a further evolution of our understanding: we emphasize how the learner can gain control of the writing process and how the instructor can guide the students' discoveries. We believe the shift, seen in this edition, from a workbook format to a brief rhetoric, will facilitate the teaching process.

The book consistently breaks down the writing process into individual tasks: each chapter, structured in the same manner, presents a task and illustrates it in a realistic writing situation; the illustration demonstrates strategies for performing that task. The chapters are both sequential and cumulative; that is, they occur in a logical learning order so that tasks and strategies are developed step by step in manageable increments. Yet this sequence can be interrupted at any chapter for special emphases, such as the instructor's introduction of supplementary, enriching materials. Reinforcement is continuous, yet adaptable to the instructor's and student's needs.

The integrated vocabulary of the book makes its new writing concepts readily accessible to students. The writing concepts and the various strategies are described in consistent, well-defined terms that are systematically related to one another. The terms themselves are performative: they convey a sense of doing and acting. And to help students analyze one another's work, these terms provide a common vocabulary for talking about writing.

Finally the structure of each chapter emphasizes the practical application of writing concepts: each chapter concludes with a section called "Applying the Concept" that directs this emphasis. Rather than making specific and inflexible assignments, this section provides many samples of the kind of writing practice that students will undertake. It suggests models of skilled writing for study and explains how students can adapt these models to their own purposes. This section concludes with several key questions to help students assess their own performances in the writing assignments. These questions, using the common vocabulary, allow class discussion that is constructive and purposeful.

In sum, this book directly addresses the complexities of writing. And by separately identifying and then relating the components of this process, it makes the teaching and learning of writing more precise, more finite, and more engaging.

We thank the following reviewers for their valuable comments: Althea M. Allard, Rhode Island Junior College; Beverly Beem, Walla Walla College; Anita Brostoff, Carnegie-Mellon University; Alma G. Bryant, University of South Florida; Beverly L. Clark, Wheaton College; Lallie J. Coy, Triton College; Peter W. Dowell, Emory University; Barbara C. Ewell, University of Mississippi; George T. Gilmore, University of Massachusetts; Josephine Giorgio, Rhode Island Junior College; Edward A. Hagan, Western Connecticut State College; Stuart Johnson, Massachusetts Institute of Technology; Wendy and Gary Lehman, formerly of Doane College; James Logue, Williamsport Area Community College; Travis Looper, McLennan Community College; Hilda M. Meyer, Triton College; Russell J. Meyer, University of Missouri-Columbia; Thomas H. Miles, West Virginia University; Frances Shirley, Wheaton College; John E. Trimpey, University of Tennessee at Chattanooga.

A. D. V.
C. H. K.
J. P.

A Forecast of the Book

What is writing? To many students, it may consist of words on a page returned by the instructor with marks in the margins. This sense of writing is limited, since there is really much more to writing that is satisfying, even exciting. This book will highlight the exciting possibilities by showing you how to write what you mean and how to do so consistently.

These possibilities pertain equally to your academic writing (exams, term papers, lab reports) and your writing for other purposes, which might include letters to the editor, job applications, minutes of meetings, business memos, magazine articles, even books. No matter what your purpose, this book presents strategies for controlling what you write and shows you how to use those strategies.

You can therefore expect to learn from this book how to discover your purposes in writing and how to achieve them, and you can expect to gain control of your writing habits. The discovery and achievement of your purposes in writing will be addressed systematically in a way that will help you demystify writing. In this introduction we will discuss the nature of writing, then we will present an overview of the book, describing the sequence of its chapters and the way in which they describe the writing process.

Again, what is writing? The meaning of the word is elusive. Sometimes it denotes a *product*—a string of sentences on a page. Sometimes it denotes a *process*—the sequence of operations or activities by which someone organized those sentences. The idea of writing as a product is important when you are concentrating on what other people have written, as you do at one time or another in most academic courses, such as philosophy, history, literature, economics, or physics. But the

1

idea of writing as a process becomes urgently important the moment you commit yourself to building a product—a written statement, such as those you read. When you study writing, in fact, your written products become the means of your understanding the process.

Writing Is Learning

The writing process is essentially *composing*, that is, the forming of relationships among pieces of information. Most of these relationships originate with you; they do not exist until you compose them. This startling fact has a fascinating consequence. Because you originate the relationship among pieces of information, your writing is thereby a means of discovering, of becoming aware of connections that you did not know until you started to compose them. To put this idea another way, you become aware of the connections you make simply by writing, and you thereby know more about your subject—whatever it may be—than you knew when you started to write about it. You acquire knowledge by writing. In one sense, knowledge is an awareness of relationships, and your growing awareness of relationships as you compose becomes your new knowledge. The process of writing is therefore a powerful way of learning.

Your learning occurs more rapidly as you write if you are trying to communicate the connections you are making. To communicate is to convey these original relationships through verbal structures that your readers can recognize and understand, that is, through sentences that make sense, through paragraphs that gather sentences together, and through sequences of paragraphs that convey some evident order. Making sense to a reader imposes certain limitations or constraints on your composing, thereby causing you to become more certain of what you mean. Your study of the writing process will reveal how these constraints actually help you to write what you mean.

The Nature of the Writer's Decisions

Since writing occurs in language, and since written language is linear, the writer's task in communicating is to control relationships among pieces of information even as those relationships are forming, one by one. The film maker faces the same problem, and so does the computer programmer. Like a written statement, both the film and the computer program are linear; they can present only a limited set of information at a time, yet the information must be continuously classified and put into some configuration while it is being conveyed so that the film viewer or the computer compiler can make sense of it. On the one hand, meaning accumulates; on the other hand, some framework for comprehending the meaning must be evident at every moment during the film or the computer program—or the written statement— if these products are to communicate.

The process of making continuous meaning differs in the film and in the computer program, but the writing process will involve you in some aspects of each. The film maker constructs a continuous line of reasoning only after the camera has photographed separate scenes relating to the subject. The major task is to edit the film footage by cutting and rearranging various scenes to form some continuity through which meaning evolves; this continuity is controlled by a framework of related ideas. The continuity of a computer program, on the other hand, must be worked out completely before it is coded in machine language. Any lapse in the continuity of meaning will cause the machine compiler to reject the commands of the program and to send back error messages to the programmer.

The writing process involves you in both of these organizing activities, that is, in planning what you write and also in editing and revising it. But writing is even more complex than film making or programming, since it entails both planning and revising while you are writing. The process of composing requires you to make many kinds of decisions, all of which bear in some way on the simple but momentous choice of what to say next.

As you will see, writing is a process of making and stating relationships; the more you know about this process, the better you can control it. Specifically, the more you know about the way to make choices when you write, the better you can make those choices suit your purpose.

This book will present you with many choices to make in the context of precise writing situations. And these situations will pose the choices in a way that will enable you to understand the decisions that you make. The purpose of this book is to show you how to analyze what you write as you are writing. If you can make this kind of analysis, you will find it relatively easy to modify any statement as you are composing it.

You will learn to analyze what you write by slowing down the process that you are engaged in and by raising questions about what you are doing as you do it. Beginning with the next chapter, you will have some elemental choices to make as you proceed through the book. The choices themselves do not become more difficult, but they do accumulate as you proceed. In later chapters you will have more choices to coordinate at any one time.

The Sequence of the Book

Each part of the book consists of a group of chapters dealing with different but related aspects of the writing process. Each chapter presents one new concept about making relationships and the decisions in which that concept will involve you. The chapters are sequential and cumulative.

Part 1, "Making Relationships," describes and illustrates the natural, exploratory process that takes place when you write. Searching for relationships is the essence of writing. What you communicate to your reader is the set of relationships you have found among pieces of information relevant to your subject. The chapters in Part 1 concentrate on the way you make these connections by writing.

Part 2, "Writing to Readers," discusses the needs and expectations of all readers. You learn about their frames of reference in order to discover how to communicate. Part 2 shows you how to use an intended reader's expectations to your own advantage and to the reader's advantage as well—even when you don't know exactly who your reader is.

All readers, of course, are different, and every reader has a unique frame of reference that must be accommodated if he or she is to understand what you are saying. On the other hand, all readers have certain traits in common. Your awareness of these traits will guide you in choosing and relating information to support your purpose. Accordingly, these chapters describe the traits of the common reader, showing you how to use such traits to anticipate questions that any intended reader is likely to ask about your statement.

By anticipating the reader's questions, you can more easily select and organize information, whether in a sentence, a paragraph, or a sequence of paragraphs. In all these contexts, the writer's strategies for conveying information are based on the reader's expectations. Accordingly, Part 3, "Developing an Extended Statement," will show you how to cluster assertions together and put those clusters in sequences that accommodate your reader's expectations. It will also show you how to forecast your intended sequence. One illustration of forecasting is the chapter that you are now reading. It describes the organizing idea of this book, the categories of information pertaining to it, and the sequence in which they will occur.

There is still more, however, to developing an extended statement. Later chapters in Part 3 will show you how to expand an extended statement as you write, that is, how to generate new relationships and make new assertions while still accommodating your reader. They will show you how to keep your reader continually informed of the changes you are making as you write.

Part 4, "Making an Extended Statement Coherent," reveals how you can develop your line of reasoning by monitoring it, thereby ensuring its continuity. It will show you how to complete your extended statement with a conclusion that represents your full discovery of what you want to say. In one sense, the conclusion is your reason for writing; it fulfills your promise to your intended reader to say something significant. It also completes your process of learning about your subject.

As you work through successive chapters of *The Process of Writing: Discovery and Control,* the concepts it presents should become clearer to you; you will see that they all relate to your own habits when you write. Knowing the concepts will enable you to control your writing habits better than you could before. You will write more coherently in less time than it now takes. That is the promise this book makes in return for your attention. By heeding the propositions in each chapter and by practicing the operations that you learn, you can fulfill this promise for yourself.

Part 1: Making Relationships

1. The Nature of Assertions

Writing is a learning process. No matter what you write—a journal, a business letter, an assigned essay, or a report—you gain new insights as you continue to compose. You discover new relationships among the pieces of information that you have gathered in order to write your statement. No matter what your subject is or how much you already know about it, you will learn more as you write. Thus writing is a process of discovery.

Writing is also a way to communicate. You start by selecting a subject, but you may not be certain about what you want to say or how to present it. You move beyond your initial hesitation and indecision as soon as you establish your first relationship. Once you have established a relationship and stated it in the form of an assertion, you then can communicate your insights to a reader.

What Is a Subject?

A **subject** is whatever focuses your attention as you write. It is that part of your environment on which you are concentrating at any given moment. This environment could include what you are experiencing, what you know, or what you recall from conversations, lectures, readings, or films. When you focus on a specific aspect of your environment—whether it be a significant learning experience, a social injustice, or a cultural event—you thereby have a subject. Your subject establishes the boundaries within which you search for information to include in your writing.

We will use the term *information* as a basic concept in this book.

8

Information consists of those data that you use in order to compose a written statement. The notes that you jot down about a subject are pieces of information. Such notes may be derived from your memory, but they may also be derived from various other sources, such as interviews, lectures, dialogues, or readings. These notes may sometimes take the form of sentences, but more often they are less than sentences; they are simply *fragments,* that is, single words or word groups. As you write, you continually discover relationships among such pieces of information.

Given any subject, you select pieces of information that relate to it and exclude those that do not. Choices about what to include or reject are guided and restricted by what you establish as the limits of your subject. For example, if the subject is "space exploration," you might select information about space satellites, astronauts, rocket fuels, or even Flash Gordon. At the same time, you would probably reject information about agriculture, nineteenth-century literature, and folk songs. Your subject shows you where to look for information: it focuses your attention, thereby simplifying your search for the raw materials of a statement.

Almost always, your subject will be too broad at first to work with effectively; it will need to be narrowed and focused. You can accomplish this preliminary focusing by jotting down bits of information about your subject: these fragments can guide you as you limit the scope of your subject. For example, if you were to choose to write about "the draft for military service," jotting down bits of information about the subject would helpfully restrict it; you might find that you do not mean to write about "the draft" but about "the draftee versus the volunteer" or "the case for drafting men and women." A limited subject is more manageable than a broad subject.

Similarly, if you were to choose "writing" as a subject, you would be starting with far too broad a concept to work with effectively. Assembling some bits of information about the subject—from your memory, your notes, a news story that you remember, or any source you wish— would show you how to restrict it. You might discover that your revised subject is really "the novelist's use of childhood memories," for example, or "the financial realities of writing for a living" or "how skilled writers revise." In selecting one of those narrower topics, you would probably decide to reject information about other possible topics, such as "the new illiteracy" or "changes in verse forms."

The usefulness of the subject itself, nevertheless, can be overestimated. Books about writing typically begin with a chapter on "discovering your subject." This book does not—for a good reason. You can name a subject, but the name by itself conveys almost no significance. You begin to see what is significant about your subject only after you have gathered information and have begun to find relationships among the pieces of information you have selected.

Finding Relationships

Discovering relationships among pieces of information is the essential activity of both the learning process and the writing process. You can understand separate ideas or concepts more precisely by associating them with other concepts to form systems of information. Each time you discover how one concept connects with another, you are learning something more specific about your subject. By discovering such a new relationship, you increase your understanding of the concepts you started with, and you also derive an additional concept that relates them.

You probably already recognize certain conventional modes of relationship as taught in many composition courses. *Classification* is the most familiar of these modes, whereby things are connected on the basis of characteristics they share. The dragon, the unicorn, and the centaur are all mythological beasts. The term *mythological beasts* denotes the class or category of relationship to which these creatures belong.

Cause and effect is another familiar mode of relationship. The terms *mosquito* and *malaria* can be related causally, since some types of mosquitoes transmit malaria. A causal connection is implicit in the expression, "where there's smoke there's fire."

A third familiar mode of relationship is *hierarchy*. A hierarchy is an arrangement of pieces of information in a series, proceeding either in increasing or decreasing order. The terms *cardinal, bishop,* and *priest,* for example, are related according to an order of rank. These terms could also be related by class, since each denotes a type of Catholic clergy. There are often several ways of relating the same information.

Such conventional modes of relationship, however, comprise only a small fraction of the relationships that you continually make. Finding relationships is a natural habit; it is the essence of your natural learning process. You do it instinctively every time you look at the world around you. Writing is simply one form of that learning process; it helps you make connections among ideas. When you make connections, you perceive that your information has a new significance. This new significance is what you communicate.

Narrowing Your Subject

Suppose you choose to write about a contemporary American "crisis." You realize that this term has been used to describe many situations or events that inconvenience or threaten people. Examples of such crises are the decreasing supply of fossil fuel, the increase of violent crime, pervasive illiteracy, and pollution from the disposal of industrial wastes. There are many others, of course. Consider mass transit, for example. Suppose you commute by means of mass transit and are concerned about recent events that might seriously inconvenience you. And suppose you, therefore, decide to write about the mass transit crisis in order to alert other citizens, especially legislators.

Your purpose requires that you make a decision; the subject is so broad that you cannot include all the information available about it. You must decide upon some way to narrow it so as to create the emphasis that you intend. A good way to begin narrowing is to list some of the information that you believe pertains to your subject. Such a list will help you establish precise relationships. Here is an example of such a list:

◇ high cost of maintenance and new equipment
◇ political overtones—taxpayers' resentment of possible increases in taxes to subsidize fares
◇ decline in federal revenues
◇ local residents' disapproval of local subsidy
◇ burden on commuter
◇ decline in service—fewer trips

This list presents a problem typical of any writing task. You have a broad subject and a collection of information, but you have not yet discovered what you want to say. Studying this list will help you establish a narrower focus for your statement. You might decide, for example, to write about "the effects of rising costs and diminishing revenues on mass transit."

But merely limiting your subject does not guarantee that you will immediately be able to write about it. You need to find a way of relating these fragments of information in order to establish a pattern. There are many different relationships that you could find among these pieces of information, and only you, as writer, can decide which relationship suits your purpose. Look again at the information:

◇ high cost of maintenance and new equipment
◇ political overtones—taxpayers' resentment of possible increases in taxes to subsidize fares
◇ decline in federal revenues
◇ local residents' disapproval of local subsidy
◇ burden on commuter
◇ decline in service—fewer trips

Suppose you now specify a relationship between mass transit and financial constraints. You might state such a relationship this way:

Rising costs and diminishing revenues threaten the continued existence of mass transit.

Notice the nature of this relationship: the sentence links "rising costs and diminishing revenues" to the "continued existence of mass transit." The precise link is furnished by the verb *threatens*, which specifies the relationship. Moreover, because this sentence asserts a relationship, it conveys what the writer considers to be significant about these information fragments.

Making Assertions: Illustration 1

Any sentence that establishes a relationship among pieces of information is an **assertion**. Throughout this book, we will refer to the assertion—a statement of relationship—as the basic unit of any written text. Since assertions establish the relationships that you believe are important, they are your means of communicating the significance of your information to your reader.

The assertion may be in the form of either a declarative sentence or a question—whichever suits your purpose. Notice that the assertion about financial strain and the continued existence of mass transit is expressed as a declarative sentence. But it can also appear as a question:

Do rising costs and diminishing revenues threaten the continued existence of mass transit?

Whether it appears in a question or a statement, the verb *threaten* relates one information fragment ("rising costs and diminishing revenues") to the other ("the continued existence of mass transit").

In the conventions of written language, a simple sentence—with a subject and its verb—is the shortest statement that conveys an explicit assertion of relationship. Isolated words or phrases convey merely *subjects:* for example, "the high cost of dying," "a case for euthanasia," or "the hospice movement and dying with dignity." But what about the high cost of dying, or euthanasia, or the hospice movement and dignity? An assertion answers this question: "What about the subject?" You cannot make an assertion about information fragments in less than a simple sentence. A subject and its verb form the basic elements of an assertion.

Making Assertions: Illustration 2

Suppose you are concerned about the natural resources of the ocean, and you want to express your concern. Your first task would be to narrow the scope of the subject "the natural resources of the ocean," which is too broad to handle effectively. As already indicated, a useful means of narrowing your subject would be to list some of the information you plan to use in your statement. These information fragments will be various, some specific and some general. But your notes, simplified, might include the following:

◇ breeding grounds of fish jeopardized by offshore drilling
◇ fish—large source of world's food supply
◇ Grand Banks as a source of oil
◇ balance of nature upset
◇ pollution of breeding grounds by oil spills
◇ serving the public interest
◇ time needed to conduct research
◇ trade-offs

After studying this information, you might choose to limit your statement to "the effects of offshore drilling on schools of fish." Once you have narrowed the focus of your subject, you can specify some relationship between offshore drilling and the breeding grounds of fish. Stating that relationship in the form of an assertion helps you increase your understanding of your subject. Many assertions could be made about this set of information fragments, but you alone can decide what you want to say.

Your first or second assertion will probably not capture exactly what you intend to convey. Your initial response, for example, might be: "Drilling for oil in the ocean could create a shortage of fish." But you may decide that this assertion does not include such information as the importance of discovering alternative sources of oil or the wisdom of conducting careful research—information that you believe is needed to convey your message. A more comprehensive assertion, one that included all the information you listed, might be: "Although drilling for oil may supply one important resource, it may also create a shortage of another equally vital resource, fish."

This complex assertion now includes all the information in the first assertion but qualifies it in such a way as to make a more comprehensive statement. This revised assertion, incidentally, can encompass all the information in your list. Now look at a paragraph that makes these connections explicit:

> Few people would censure recent attempts to find alternative sources of oil. Once discovered, these sources could serve the public by helping to prevent future shortages. But the careless retrieval of oil could also do a disservice to the public, especially if it has a detrimental effect on another equally vital resource, fish. The offshore drilling for oil on the Grand Banks is a case in point. Schools of fish, which breed in such areas, are a significant source of the world's food supply. Pollution of breeding grounds by oil spills could upset the balance of nature, resulting in a serious shortage of this source of food. Before any drilling is done, therefore, careful research must be undertaken. Only then will we have a good understanding of the long-range effects of such drilling and of how wise it is to trade off the destruction of breeding grounds for an increased supply of oil.

There are many assertions that you or another writer might derive from the same set of information. Someone might assert, for example, that "the benefits of offshore drilling are offset by its disadvantages." Had you chosen to make this assertion, you would probably develop a stronger statement against drilling for oil on breeding grounds.

Summary

Writing is a learning process. As you think about your subject, you gather pieces of information about it. As you select pieces of information, you look for relationships among them. Gathering and connecting items of information causes you to learn about your subject. The relationships that you make are what you want to communicate. Think of stating these relationships by means of assertions—that is, by means of sentences that specify relationships among information fragments. Assertions reveal the significance of your information, thereby making your writing more meaningful and more accessible to your readers.

Applying the Concept: Making Relationships

This chapter has described activities involved in virtually any writing task. To start writing, you collect raw material in the form of notes; you search for relationships among these bits of information; then you state the relationships you have discovered. You continue the process of searching for relationships and stating them in the sentences and paragraphs that follow.

By practicing these activities of searching and stating without worrying at this point about whether your sentences are correct, you can reduce the time it takes to get started on any writing task. Grammatical correctness is important, of course, since it helps you convey more precisely whatever you are trying to express, but deliberate editing for correctness comes later, after you have produced a series of related assertions. To start building a string of assertions that can form a paragraph, the first task is to assemble bits of information that you think might pertain to your subject. The discovery process begins with your search for clusters of information.

Pick a subject that interests you, one you might like to explore, and start to generate a list of information about it: its colors, shapes, abstract qualities, or your attitude toward it—or whatever comes to mind when you think about the subject. For purposes of practice, any subject that interests you will do; pick one quickly—a nearby object that you can describe or something that you can easily imagine—and start your list. What about an island, for example? A more limited and probably more interesting subject might be "an unpopulated island," or even better, "living on an unpopulated island." Here is one possible list of items of information that pertain to your subject:

◇ supplies—food and fresh water
◇ protection from sun and rain
◇ cold nights
◇ loneliness
◇ passing the time

◇ exploring
◇ Robinson Crusoe
◇ tools
◇ adventure and discovery
◇ signals and messages

What other information could you list about such an island that would pertain to living there? Think of psychological as well as physical needs. One or two items on your list will tend to suggest others: things that you have read about or remember or can imagine. Continue listing until you have ten or twelve items; then scan the list, allowing the items you have already listed to lead you to new ones. Searching for information usually proceeds by your making free associations, a natural habit for everyone. You will also be making such associations when you begin to search for relationships or patterns among the items on the list.

Try list making as a game, and practice it whenever you have a couple of minutes to spare. Make several lists, as if you were preparing to write a statement. Suppose you choose as a subject the geometric shapes that you can see repeated in the objects around you. Or think of important calendar dates and the occasions they bring to mind, preparations for a trip, or even a shopping list of items you have been meaning to buy. Then pick any one of your lists and start to search for relationships among the items.

There are various ways to proceed in making relationships. One way is to look for two items that seem to be related and then name some element they have in common. Using this common element, search for other items on the list that could be related to it in one way or another. After you have searched the list for all the items related to the first element, try the procedure again to see how many of the remaining items you can link to a second common element. Or you may discover that you can scan the whole list and intuitively organize the items without taking separate steps. Don't bother to use all the items on the list; concentrate on only those items that are easiest to link.

Once most of the items on your list are organized by common elements, relate these items explicitly by writing assertions. Each assertion, of course, will contain a verb that specifies a relationship among information fragments. Make the assertion answer the question "What about these items?" Given any two or three items, you will probably be able to make several assertions within a few minutes. Think in terms of the ideas represented by the words on your list, and do not limit your-

self to using only those words you have already used. Confining yourself to the original words will often limit your ability to make more precise relationships.

  After some experimenting, you will probably find that you can make
several assertions that relate the items on your list in different ways,
even those items that share a common element. If you work at the
process with other students, you will be able to generate still more lists
and more assertions. Given any subject, for example, "television viewing," how many lists can you make together? Given any list, how many
assertions can you make using the procedure already described?

  If your subject were television viewing, you would begin by listing
information fragments about your subject:

◇ entertainment standards
◇ silence is golden
◇ enjoyment of whatever you like
◇ educational television
◇ aimed at mentality of twelve-year-old child

Look for some common element, or principle of relationship, that connects any two or more of these items, and use that principle to combine
those items into an assertion; combine them by means of a verb. Here
are some possible assertions:

  Educational television provides a useful alternative to the general
  fare.

  People spend hours watching television, without considering the low
  standards of the entertainment they watch.

  Since the standards of entertainment on television are so low, some
  people refuse to turn on their sets, insisting that silence is golden.

  People have the right to watch whatever they like, despite the opinions of others.

  As we said, you need not repeat the actual words in the items on the
list; the concepts are what you build with. Here is an example that relates concepts suggested by items on the list, yet does not include the
specific words themselves:

  Since viewers can change the channel or turn off the set whenever they wish, they have complete control over television.

In the final paper, some of these assertions will be more useful than
others. Usually, the most useful assertions are the most comprehen-

sive—those that provide you with the most possibilities for continuing. Scan your assertions: which ones can you build on and which ones should you discard?

With the guidelines of Chapter 1 in mind, you and your classmates might want to discuss the assertions that you have all written to see if they convey the intended relationships as clearly as possible. The following questions might help your discussion:

1. How is any one piece of information related to the others?
2. Do all information fragments in the assertion help support or modify the declared relationship?
3. Which information fragment in each assertion seems to you to be the most promising point of departure for making further assertions?

2. The Writer's Organizing Idea

In Chapter 1, we stated that an assertion establishes and clarifies relationships among separate pieces of information. An assertion, expressed as a sentence, conveys the significance of that information. But you usually make more than one assertion when you are composing; you usually write a series of assertions. When you are trying to communicate two or more sentences, therefore, your task is to organize your assertions into a unified statement.

This chapter focuses on the task of composing a paragraph. The paragraph is a group of related sentences; more precisely, it is a group of assertions related to each other in a way that helps both the reader and the writer. In order to follow and to understand any extended series of assertions that you may write, your reader needs some means of relating them to each other. Similarly, at any given time in the process of composing successive assertions, you need a way of relating what you have written to what you are about to write. The easiest means of helping both you and your reader in this case is to group assertions in some way or other.

Writers may use many different ways of relating successive assertions to one another. The form of any one assertion offers the writer certain choices in—and certain limits to—forming the next assertion. As you write, you make such choices, causing a new assertion to follow what you have just written. This continuity is necessary if your reader is to understand what you are writing. Continuity by itself, however, is not enough to provide your reader with a unified statement. For example, your ninth assertion may follow easily from the eighth, but do they both follow from your second assertion? Your reader needs to know the overall relationship of these assertions, and you can meet this need by grouping successive assertions so that they relate to one overall assertion. When you group your assertions in this way, you are composing a paragraph.

You can think of a paragraph, therefore, as a series of assertions that are related to each other in two different ways, both of which are necessary if the paragraph is to become a unified statement. Each assertion is related in some manner to the one that precedes it or to the one that follows it. And all of the assertions are related in some manner to one central assertion.

We will refer to this one central assertion as an organizing idea because it organizes separate assertions into a paragraph. This term is important. An **organizing idea** is itself an assertion, but specifically it is an assertion that unifies other assertions. Finding the organizing idea for successive assertions is one of the writer's primary tasks. And, although this may seem surprising, finding organizing ideas is one of the important reasons for writing. As you evaluate your information, you search for a way to organize it. Whenever you are trying to say what you mean, chances are you are trying to discover an organizing idea.

In later chapters we will describe how you can make an organizing idea connect and regulate a whole series of paragraphs. But you can exercise such control only after first understanding how an organizing idea functions to make separate assertions form a paragraph, which is why this chapter focuses on the paragraph.

Deriving an Organizing Idea

Suppose that you have recently encountered a member of a religious cult. She has made some carefully formulated statements about the advantages of joining a cult, and those statements have encouraged you to think about the subject. Perhaps you are not sure of your own opinion about cults, since so many different opinions about such cults exist. Some people, for example, accuse religious cults of being fraudulent and their leaders of being kidnappers; others say that cults fulfill an important spiritual need by providing strength and reinforcement to their members. Divided opinions such as these often occur. Because controversy persists, let us assume that the subject continues to intrigue you. Your interest leads you to explore the conflicting values pertaining to religious cults so you can clarify your own view.

You already know how to begin exploring your subject. As we indicated in Chapter 1, you can assemble a list of information fragments relevant to religious cults. Try to remember what you have heard or read, and list the items as they occur to you. Here is a possible list:

◇ historical background of cultism
◇ traditional religions
◇ psychological problems
◇ indoctrination and brainwashing
◇ cults provide friendship and support
◇ alienation from family
◇ common goals for cult members
◇ cult leaders evade taxes
◇ sense of identity
◇ difficult re-entry into society
◇ sacrificing money and possessions to a cult
◇ group decision making

You could probably add other pieces of information to this list, but these are enough to illustrate how you can derive an organizing idea for a paragraph about your subject.

Cults have many aspects, of course, and attempting to discuss all these aspects in one paragraph would result at best in the recitation of mere generalities. It is necessary to narrow the subject before starting your paragraph, which will allow you to concentrate on the aspect that interested you or engaged you in the first place. The list of information you have assembled offers a guide to narrowing the subject. Glancing back at the list, you can probably see one common element right away: some of the information fragments favor cults and others do not. The controversy itself might be an appropriate subject for a paragraph, specifically, "conflicting opinions about cults."

At this point it is useful to pause and reflect on the way this common element came into being. "Conflicting opinions about cults" is not itself an item on the list. The writer had to derive it or, to use another word, to infer it. You can infer more than one common element from any list of information, and that common element almost always occurs in your mind; no one item on a list wholly provides it. This observation is important because it also explains how you derive any assertion—that is, any statement of relationship, including an organizing idea. The organizing idea that you infer from any list of information depends solely on the way you perceive that information.

Creating Your Own Organizing Idea

By glancing again at the information about cults, you can see how this process works. (The process, incidentally, is called *inference*.) Some of the items on this list, such as "psychological problems" and "alienation from family," are merely information fragments. You can identify the others that are also fragments.

◇ historical background of cultism
◇ traditional religions
◇ psychological problems
◇ indoctrination and brainwashing
◇ cults provide friendship and support
◇ alienation from family
◇ common goals for cult members
◇ cult leaders evade taxes
◇ sense of identity
◇ difficult re-entry into society
◇ sacrificing money and possessions to a cult
◇ group decision making

As we pointed out in Chapter 1, such pieces of information by themselves convey almost no significance. The writer gives them significance by inferring some relationship among the information fragments and then stating an assertion that specifies that relationship.

Your task as a writer is always to build relationships. Sometimes you will even be building a relationship between two other relationships; you will be interrelating pieces of information, which is what happens when one assertion follows another. You may already have noted, for example, that two items on the list are already assertions; they are complete sentences.

◇ Cults provide friendship and support.
◇ Cult leaders evade taxes.

Since each of them already states a relationship, you could decide to include either or both in your paragraph, although you might have to modify the sentence form so that each assertion follows smoothly from the one preceding it.

But our emphasis at this point is on deriving an organizing idea from a list of information fragments. As we said earlier, you could derive different assertions from the list about cults. One way to go about the task would be to write several assertions and compare them to see which one seems to gather and organize most of the information on the list. Or you might prefer to compose several assertions mentally, without writing them down, discarding each assertion until you are satisfied with one that fits your sense of how to incorporate the information into a paragraph.

Recall the subject of cults, which we narrowed earlier to "conflicting opinions about cults." You could make inferences from various combinations of items on the list until you could state an assertion that would help you organize your information. One such assertion might be this:

> One must study the conflicting opinions about cults before making an informed statement about them.

This might do for an organizing idea, although it seems rather dull; it doesn't say very much. By experimenting, you could probably find a more promising organizing idea. Testing one assertion to see if it will serve as an organizing idea often suggests another. Here, for example, are two assertions that make bolder claims than the first one; they state different opinions, but either one would give you a good chance to develop your ideas.

> Some individuals can happily subject themselves to the group solidarity that cults promise.
>
> Group solidarity in a cult may exist only at great cost to the individual.

Any of these three assertions could organize all the items—both the fragments and the assertions—on the information list; that is, you could use the items on the list to support and extend whichever assertion you choose to be the organizing idea.

When you start to write, the order in which you make the assertions is also a matter of your own choice. You could start with your organizing idea, you could conclude with it, or you could state it somewhere in the paragraph. In each case, you are stating your organizing idea explicitly. But you need not state the organizing idea at all. Surprising as this may sound, you can make all the assertions on the page relate to the organizing idea in your mind without even stating that organizing idea for your reader. This possibility is valid because your reader, like you, can also make inferences. If you have kept your organizing idea in mind while writing the paragraph, your reader will be able to follow the assertions you have written and then make an assertion that is very close to your organizing idea.

Skilled writers often imply an organizing idea instead of stating it. By implying it, they gain flexibility; they can explore a subject as they write and discover relationships they were unaware of when they started. This possibility of implying an organizing idea is so important to writers that it deserves to be emphasized. In traditional rhetoric, the organizing idea of a paragraph is often called a *topic sentence*. Although any good paragraph contains some organizing principle, not all paragraphs contain topic sentences. *Organizing idea*, therefore, is a more accurate term than *topic sentence* because an organizing idea is not limited to being explicitly stated. An organizing idea may actually occur as one of the sentences in a paragraph, or it may be implied by the other assertions.

There is one other important difference between a topic sentence and an organizing idea. Unlike a topic sentence, an organizing idea is not static. It begins in your consciousness as an impression of the probable relationships you will establish. This impression is often tentative at first. It is your best estimate of the significance of your information, and it grows progressively clearer to you as you write. You come to recognize your organizing idea more fully only through your effort to relate it to your information. The notion of a topic sentence denies the possibility of growth or development. It assumes that a writer has already found a fully evolved idea. But in most paragraphs, the developed organizing idea is an achievement of the writing process, not a ready-made conclusion at the start.

Here is a summary of what has been said so far about an organizing idea:

◇ An organizing idea is an assertion you formulate in your own mind.
◇ It begins as an estimate of the significance of your information, and it develops as you write.
◇ It is an assertion that will enable you to relate and unify all the information in your paragraph.
◇ It is a logical component of your finished paragraph, whether or not it actually occurs as a sentence.

Testing the Paragraph

To review what we said at the beginning of this chapter, a paragraph is a group of assertions that are related in two ways. One kind of relationship concerns their continuity, and the other concerns their unity. The continuity of assertions within a paragraph is the simpler relationship and the easier one to test. Given the first assertion, each one thereafter follows in some evident way from those that precede it. As a paragraph proceeds, each assertion adds new information and new relationships to the related information already stated.

The way to test a paragraph for continuity, while reading it, is to question whether the new information follows in some evident way from the information already in place. The continuity of assertions, however, does not depend on mere surface connections, as the following example makes clear. Each assertion appears at first glance to follow its predecessor, yet notice the drift from one subject to another.

> Religious cults have flourished in all societies. In societies, social groups as well as religious groups include people with similar interests who wish to share their leisure activities. Leisure, which is becoming more important in many societies, can be devoted to spectator activities as well as participant activities. Spectator activities include watching sports, and there are many new sports that are now available to spectators, thanks to television. Indeed, television has become an important source of knowledge to people of all ages, and knowledge makes progress possible.

This series of assertions reflects merely the writer's free association of ideas. If you look at the first and last sentences in the series, you can see how far the later assertions have drifted from the first statement of relationship. The successive assertions provide no continuity of relationship; therefore, they do not form a paragraph.

You recall that a paragraph is a group of assertions that are related by their continuity and by their unity. As you can probably see after the last example, the continuity of assertions depends on their being unified; that is, it depends on their all relating to some central assertion that can sustain them. This mutual relationship, wherein all assertions relate to one central assertion, to one organizing idea, is the unity that we speak of in a paragraph. In fact, such unity is the essential condition of a paragraph.

Without an organizing idea, the assertions in a statement remain logically unrelated. Here is what can happen when a paragraph lacks an organizing idea. Consider the following group of sentences about space exploration. It masquerades as a paragraph, but do you see why it is not a paragraph?

Babylonian astronomers were among the first to look at the sky and wonder about the stars. Space satellites have told us much about the physical composition and temperature of many of the planets in our solar system. In Galileo's time, the study of astronomy was called optics, and the first telescopes were crude. Soon unmanned vehicles will land on other planets and conduct scientific experiments.

The statement is unsatisfactory because the four assertions are unrelated to one another. Even though they all fall within the boundaries of the subject, they fail to convey any single significance. In other words, they lack an organizing idea. They cannot be summarized in a sentence.

You can test the relationship among assertions by asking this question: Do all the assertions relate to one central assertion, that is, to one organizing idea—either stated or implied? If the assertions do not all relate to a single organizing idea, then some kind of revision will be necessary to convert those assertions into a paragraph.

The most reliable test of any paragraph you have written is to try to summarize it in a single sentence. If you can, the paragraph does have an organizing idea; the assertions are mutually related. Your summary sentence is, in fact, the most developed statement of that organizing idea.

Revising the Organizing Idea

Consider the importance of this basic test of a paragraph. If, after writing a paragraph, you can summarize it in a sentence, you have thereby demonstrated that the paragraph has an organizing idea—even if the paragraph itself did not state it. This test indicates that the organizing idea evolved as you wrote the paragraph. In other words, the process of writing caused you to develop—to refine and clarify—relationships among the pieces of information about your subject.

So far in this book we have been suggesting in various ways that writing is an act of discovery. Making assertions about any subject causes you to learn more precisely what you want to express. You become more aware of what you want to say, and you naturally revise as you continue to write. Revision is a means of refining and developing any statement.

Experienced writers often deliberately evoke the discovery process by writing successive drafts of a statement. Each new draft is a revision of what is already written; specifically, the revision replaces a tentative statement of relationship with a more developed—a more precise and more complex—statement of that relationship. In other words, a developed organizing idea says more than the tentative organizing idea said.

The following example demonstrates how a writer can deliberately make use of a paragraph summary, that is, of a developed organizing idea, as a means of exploring the subject further. This procedure consists of writing a paragraph, deriving a developed organizing idea, and then using that developed organizing idea as the tentative organizing idea for another paragraph. This particular example concerns a series of paragraphs about the sport of parachuting. The writer begins by questioning why anyone would want to parachute and then evolves some answers to the question.

SUBJECT

parachuting as a sport

LIST OF INFORMATION

◇ possibility of injury or death
◇ complete sense of freedom
◇ feeling of transcendence, living at the height of awareness
◇ enjoyment of danger

TENTATIVE ORGANIZING IDEA

Parachuting has some strange appeal.

PARAGRAPH

Someone would have to be crazy to jump from an airplane. Yet skyjumping has appealing aspects. There seems to be a sense of freedom that comes from soaring in the air and a feeling of transcendence in escaping the earth's bonds. There is also a sense of challenge in allowing one's life to depend on the durability of a few yards of silk.

DEVELOPED ORGANIZING IDEA

It would seem that skyjumpers are insane, yet the sport appeals to those who are looking for freedom, transcendence, and challenge.

Now see how this developed organizing idea can serve as a basis for developing the writer's ideas even further. Specifically, the writer can use it as a tentative organizing idea of another paragraph that will refine and extend the relationships in the earlier paragraphs.

REVISED PARAGRAPH

Leaping from an airplane seems a species of madness. Yet parachuting for sport is growing more popular every day. One reason is the sense of freedom that comes from soaring thousands of feet in the air. Another reason may be one's feeling of transcendence in slipping "the surly bonds of earth." But there must also be an underlying love of danger, a need to live "right at the edge" before life can be truly enjoyed, that distinguishes the skyjumper from most other sports enthusiasts. It is this fundamental thirst for danger that pushes the skyjumpers out of the door, high above the ground, their lives depending on the durability of a few yards of silk.

DEVELOPED ORGANIZING IDEA 2

The skyjumper is a special breed of sports enthusiast who values above all else the sense of danger, the special exhilaration associated with the sport.

Can you see how the second developed organizing idea represents the writer's most significant assertion? In the revised paragraph, the writer has asserted that the third reason, the thirst for danger, is more important than the other two reasons, freedom and transcendence. Rewriting a statement expands your knowledge of your subject. It also sharpens your awareness of your organizing idea. Notice that the writer has implied the developed organizing idea rather than stating it explicitly.

Summary

You begin to organize your writing as you become aware of the significance of your assertions. When you have discovered a single assertion that unifies all the assertions in a paragraph, you have a way to organize those assertions. This single assertion is your tentative organizing idea. As you write, it evolves into a developed organizing idea, that is, the most important assertion about your subject.

Applying the Concept: The Writer's Organizing Idea

A paragraph makes sense by effectively conveying an organizing idea to the reader. In fact, what a skilled reader chiefly remembers about any paragraph is its major idea, not the subordinate ideas that develop it. You can improve your reading skills, and also learn more about what an organizing idea does, by inferring the organizing idea in any paragraph that you read.

As an exercise, read a short magazine article or an essay in your composition reader. Then return to its first paragraph and reread it. Can you infer the organizing idea of that paragraph? Write down a complete sentence rather than a fragment. Ask other people what they have inferred as the organizing idea of the same paragraph and compare versions.

Now reread the second paragraph and write down its organizing idea. Continue through all the paragraphs in the essay, comparing your inferences, if you wish, with those of classmates. When you have finished, your list of consecutive organizing ideas—one from each paragraph—will be a helpful outline of the essay's argument. The procedure of inferring and writing down organizing ideas, incidentally, can be a useful study aid whenever you want to remember something you have read.

Working through the following task will help you to use the concept of the organizing idea in your own writing. Choose a subject, assemble a list of information about it, and write a paragraph based on that information. You will have completed the task when you can write a sentence that accurately summarizes the paragraph, thereby proving that your paragraph has an organizing idea.

You will probably find it easier to choose a subject that allows you to express yourself, to state your opinion or your feelings. You may want to write this paragraph as a journal entry; such entries allow you to resolve perplexing situations that are part of your everyday experiences. Or you may want to write several paragraphs in a letter, describing some significant or moving event to a friend. Or you may want to describe or narrate some exhilarating experience you have had. Try to write about something that interests you; your writing will probably be livelier and more persuasive if you care about what you are saying. Did you recently have an experience, for example, that you want to describe to several friends to hear what their reactions will be? In any case, remember that this is your opportunity to express yourself. Rather than repeating someone else's ideas, you should try to create your own unique and personal view of the subject you choose.

Careful planning before you write will probably save you time in the long run. There is no right or wrong way to plan, but it is useful to remember that the writing process involves both the gathering of information and the generating of assertions. You may find it easier to list information first and then to begin to make assertions about it. Or you may begin with an assertion or two, gradually adding to the information on which your first assertions are based. It is possible that your planning will be composed of both activities at the same time, the listing of information and the making of assertions, which will in turn suggest new information to you. Continue these procedures until you have an assertion that can be used as a tentative organizing idea, one that connects four or five pieces of information. You can then begin to write your paragraph.

You might want to think about the following questions. They will help you assess your writing after you have generated your first draft. They will also guide any revision by helping you make your writing more precise.

1. Is there an explicit organizing idea in the paragraph?
2. If there is not an explicit organizing idea, is one implied?
3. Can your first developed organizing idea usefully serve as a tentative organizing idea for a new draft?
4. Are all the assertions in the paragraph clearly related to one another?
5. Are all the assertions related to one central assertion that may be stated or implied?
6. Can the paragraph be summarized in a single sentence?

After you have completed your revision, you may want to share your writing with your classmates. Talking about your writing can be useful, and sharing your writing with others will help you generate new ideas. You might come to see your writing and the writing of your classmates as your unique gifts to one another, your way of learning more about yourself and your colleagues.

3. The Writer's Purpose

In Chapter 2 we described a developed organizing idea as an assertion that relates all the other assertions in a paragraph or a longer statement. You may deliberately assign an explicit assertion to this role, or you may allow the reader to infer your organizing idea. In either case, the main assertion clarifies the significance of your information on a subject. Of course, there are many possible relationships and, therefore, many possible organizing ideas that can relate the items in any list of information. Different writers might use the same materials in different ways, and even the same writer might organize them differently on two separate occasions.

The organizing idea you choose depends on what you think is significant at the time you are writing, and how you estimate the significance of your information is influenced directly by your purposes for writing. You look for materials and organizing principles that reflect what you want to accomplish. Whatever purpose motivates you to write also influences virtually every choice you make in selecting and ordering ideas.

What Is the Writer's Purpose?

A **purpose** is simply a motive or reason for carrying out a task. When you act with a purpose, your behavior is intentional rather than random: you set a goal and try to reach it. Knowing the goal enables you to organize your actions so that they are consistent and effective. When you write, a sense of intention directs your decisions about what to say and where and how to say it. Experienced writers do not ordinarily be-

gin without cause or direction. Instead, they have purposes for starting
to write, and they use those purposes to guide the process of discovering and stating relationships.

Here is a simple instance of purposeful writing. Imagine that friends
are coming to visit but that you cannot be home when they arrive. You
might decide to leave a note saying that you will be back soon and that
they should make themselves comfortable. In this common situation,
your writing has a purpose, or probably several purposes. One goal
might be to explain your unavoidable absence and to indicate when
you will return. Another might be to tell your friends where they can
find the key you have left for them. A third might be to encourage
them to feel at home, to drink a beer, to use your stereo, to sample the
cheese in your refrigerator. We call these *communicative* purposes because they guide you in conveying a message you want your readers to
understand.

But other motives, which we can refer to as *expressive* purposes, also
direct your writing. These purposes have more to do with a writer's
self-image than with the overt message of a statement. For example,
you probably want your readers to view you in a certain way, in this
case, as a friendly, likable person. You may also want to assure them
that your absence is not a sign of thoughtlessness or indifference on
your part. You accomplish such purposes not only by what you say, the
facts you convey, but also by the way you express yourself, your style,
choice of words, and tone of voice.

Nearly all writing, even this simple note to your friends, seeks to
achieve many goals, both communicative and expressive. Being aware
of your diverse purposes will make a writing task intentional and
therefore easier: you will have something to say and also an impression
of how to say it. In this instance, the tone of your note would probably
be informal and friendly, perhaps even excited. Your choice of words
is likely to be casual or colloquial. The message you communicate
would emphasize details about your absence and instructions for your
friends. You would probably make the note brief, coming quickly to
the point without elaborate introduction or conclusion. And you would
be able to make all these choices quite easily, not because writing itself
is such a simple task, but because you know clearly what this particular
statement is intended to accomplish. The note you might leave for
friends could look like this:

Dear Milt and Jackie,
    Welcome to Pascagoula! I'm sorry I can't be here to meet you,
but—can you believe it?—I just got a call from Fred to come

downtown and meet him at a garage. His car collapsed again and had to be towed off the highway—same old Fred. I'll give you the sordid details when we get back, which should be in an hour or so.

Meantime, the key is taped under the mailbox. Pour yourselves some beer and turn on the stereo. (If you break it, you're in trouble!) We'll be home in no time. I can hardly wait to see you!

Diane

(P.S. Dinner's on Fred.)

In the case of this note, your purposes for writing are apparent, so the task of choosing what to say is easy. Any time you write, you should ask yourself about the communicative and expressive goals you wish to achieve.

Using Purposes to Direct Your Writing

Knowing what you want to accomplish helps you in the process of searching for an organizing idea. It also guides the stating of assertions that express relationships you have perceived within a range of information. Suppose, for instance, that you have purchased some new book shelves from a mail-order catalogue. On the order form, you had asked for three eight-foot shelves, stained light brown. But when the shelves arrive, you discover that they are not the ones you ordered. Instead, they are six feet long and stained a garish purple. In addition, you find that you have been charged an extra five dollars for delivery, although you had not noticed any delivery charge indicated in the catalogue. Naturally, you are annoyed that your order has been mishandled, but you are also eager to get the book shelves you requested. So you decide to write a letter.

Suppose you have sorted your information into the following categories, although you are not yet sure that you will use all the items:

1. facts about what you ordered and when
2. facts about the merchandise you actually received
3. statements about what you regard as an erroneous five-dollar handling charge
4. statements about the store's obligation to pay the cost of returning the incorrect merchandise
5. assertions about your irritation at the mistakes

6. assertions about the store's obligation to send you what you ordered
   and at the cost stated in the catalogue

Now what will you choose as an organizing idea? The answer depends on how you perceive your various purposes for writing, that is, the priority you assign to different goals. Is your primary intention to explain what has happened? Or is it to express your irritation? Or is it to repair the mistake as quickly as possible? Of course, you may wish the letter to accomplish all these ends, but some of them may be more important than others. Suppose that your decision, at least for the first draft, is to emphasize irritation at the store for mishandling your order. Given this controlling purpose, one possible organizing idea might be: "Your company has bungled my order in addition to overcharging me, and I'm annoyed about it."

You would then probably emphasize assertions based on the information in items 1, 2, 3, and 5 in order to express annoyance. It is possible, for instance, to establish a chain of relationships describing, first, the order you initially placed, then the fact that the wrong merchandise was sent, then the fact that you were incorrectly charged, and finally your feeling that the store is responsible. Meanwhile, your tone will express irritation.

But as you write for the purpose of revealing anger, and as you develop the organizing idea that expresses it, you may begin to have second thoughts. Is the full expression of your feelings really more important than the more practical intention of arguing that you are entitled to the merchandise you ordered? If you describe your annoyance so forcefully that it merely creates hostility without clarifying your desire to obtain the right book shelves at the specified price, do you improve or diminish the chances of getting what you want? Sometimes one purpose is at odds with another, and you must decide on your priorities before you can write.

Suppose you decide, in a new draft of your letter, that the more pragmatic goal of requesting the correct bookshelves has priority over the expression of feelings. But once you adjust your primary purpose, you naturally must make other adjustments as well. First, you revise your tentative organizing idea, possibly to read like this: "Since you have sent me the wrong book shelves and incorrectly charged for them, would you please rectify the error and send me what I ordered?" Then you will probably select different assertions, emphasizing those based on the information in items 4 and 6 above. You may still express annoyance, of course, but only as subordinate to your main purpose. You might even decide to reveal less irritation than you really feel in order to improve the chance that service will be speedy. The letter you finally mail to the company might look like this:

> On September 12, I ordered from your fall catalogue three eight-foot book shelves in a light brown stain. Today, I received a shipment from you, but unfortunately it contains three six-foot shelves stained in purple, clearly not the ones I requested. Moreover, you have charged me five dollars for delivery despite the fact that your catalogue, as far as I can tell, makes no mention of extra charges.
>
> I am returning the incorrect merchandise, and I assume that you will reimburse me for the shipping charges. But since I am still eager to receive the shelves I originally ordered, may I ask you to send them as soon as possible? As for the unexpected handling charge, while I am not necessarily determined to cancel my order if required to pay it, I am disturbed that you would add such a charge without advertising it in advance.
>
> I would appreciate your attending to this matter, and I look forward to receiving my bookshelves some time soon.

Notice that expressive purposes inform this letter as well as communicative ones. The writer strives to create the self-image of a firm but reasonable person, rather irked at receiving the wrong merchandise but still willing to do business, provided the mail-order company lives up to its obligations. The tone of the letter is formal but not hostile: the writer wishes to appear fair-minded (even concerning the wrongly assessed delivery fee) but without seeming to be timid or willing to accept mistreatment. The coordination of various communicative and expressive aims helps to shape the writer's organizing idea and the kinds of assertions that comprise the writing.

Imagine now that you do not get a satisfactory response from the mail-order company. Weeks pass and you receive neither the requested merchandise nor any acknowledgement of the first letter. So you decide to write a second one. It is likely that your purposes are now different, that you want to cancel the order and retrieve your money. Your annoyance is probably greater than before, and you may even suspect fraud. New purposes, in this case, lead to new choices about what to say and how to say it. Your primary communicative purpose may now be to inform the company of your demands and to state the possible consequences of continued delay. At the same time, one expressive purpose may be to reveal yourself as justifiably angry and resolved to take action, a person not to be trifled with. Just as before, the choices you make in drafting this more sharply worded letter will depend on the pressure you feel to accommodate a variety of intentions, both communicative and expressive, as the writing develops. Your awareness of your changing intent continues to govern the process of composing.

How Purpose Affects Revision

Only the simplest and most informal writing is completed in a single draft. Ordinarily, even highly skilled writers compose several drafts before they are satisfied that they have said exactly what they wanted in the clearest possible way. The necessity for multiple drafts stems from the fact that writing is a learning process. It involves tentativeness, especially at the start. You discover a developed significance only gradually, as the result of trial and error. First drafts, therefore, are usually both hardest to write and most likely to need rewriting. Later drafts complete the learning process that a first draft has begun.

But the question arises, how does a writer know when a statement is complete or when additional composing is necessary? The answer is that any statement may be considered finished when it adequately achieves the purposes for which it is written. Any statement is incomplete and needs further development when it does not yet adequately achieve its writer's purposes.

When composing a note for visiting friends, as in the example cited earlier, you may attain your goals with very little or no revision. Since the note is informal, and your friends know you, and the message is straightforward, your statement may not even require developed paragraphs in order to accomplish its ends.

But the situation is different in the letter to the mail-order company. Here, your purpose is to communicate to an intended reader who does not know you and who may not see things the way you do. You will have to convey your meaning more fully and carefully than you would to a friend. Assertions will have to be more precisely stated and interrelated to make your argument persuasive and to avoid confusion. If the intended reader cannot understand what you wish to say, then you cannot achieve your objectives.

It is likely that the precision and clarity you need in such a letter will come only gradually, perhaps after you rewrite it several times. In that case, the process of revision goes on until you are confident that your

purposes have been served, that is, until the discrepancy between what
you ordered and what the company sent has been adequately described, your irritation has been expressed, and, above all, your arguments about deserving the right merchandise at the stated price have
been clearly presented. Of course, the reader at the mail-order company may ultimately understand your statement and still take no action. You cannot control another person's behavior merely by writing.
But you will have accomplished your purposes if the reader at least un-
derstands your intent and your demands. Once you are reasonably certain that the reader will reach this understanding, you may regard
your writing as complete.

Summary

Composing begins with a sense of purpose. Only when you have decided what you want your writing to accomplish can you begin to make
choices about what to say. Having an end in mind enables you to select
and interrelate pieces of information. Your purposes guide your discovery of an organizing idea as well as the development of that idea in
successive assertions.

Your awareness of purpose also guides your rewriting: you continue
to make new choices and to revise until you are confident that the written statement accomplishes your purposes. Remember that a statement
is incomplete as long as it fails to serve the objectives that have given
rise to it.

Applying the Concept: The Writer's Purpose

You can often reconstruct a writer's intentions by looking closely at a
finished statement. For instance, you might reread a letter you have
received or a magazine article that interested you in order to estimate
the purposes of the author. Does the writer stress communicative or
expressive aims? Is one purpose to offer information? What kinds? Is
another aim to persuade you in some way? If so, how? Is any effort
made to get you to do something or believe something or behave in a
certain way? Can you see any connection between the way the information is presented and the emotional effect the writer seeks? What

self-image does the writer seek to project? Can you find other purposes? Once you are aware of them all, do you feel more inclined or less inclined to give your assent to the statement?

Working through a problem like the following one will help you use the concept of purpose in your own writing. Your instructor may suggest a different problem based on this model or encourage you to build your own. You will have solved the problem when you show that you can (1) decide on priorities among different purposes, (2) discover an organizing idea that reflects those priorities, and (3) develop the organizing idea that accomplishes your purposes.

Select some subject (for instance, "smoking marijuana" or "women in the military" or "an interesting person I've known" or "how to succeed in modeling").

1. State at least three purposes that will direct your writing, listed in order of importance. For instance, do you want to inform? Do you want to create an attitude? Do you want to be humorous? Do you want to sell an idea? Do you want to move people to do something or behave in a certain way? Do you want to be irreverent?
2. Write a paragraph developing the main idea.

Imagine, for instance, that you want to invite a noted but controversial political figure to speak at your school or club. You might discuss with your classmates all the things you would want the letter of invitation to accomplish, listing your various goals on a blackboard or sheet of paper. Certainly, an obvious goal would be to attract the speaker to your group. You would probably want to portray your school or club, and yourself as well, in a favorable light. (How might you achieve this end?) You might also want to explain why it would be especially valuable to have this speaker rather than another. That is, you might decide to flatter the proposed speaker or at least emphasize the person's particular appropriateness to the occasion you have in mind. You might also want to suggest, generally or specifically, the topic to be addressed. Since the person is somewhat controversial, you might want either to encourage or to restrict the possibility of an emotional response from the audience. Can you think of other purposes as well?

Once you have a list of goals, assess the priorities you want to establish among them. Does achieving any one of them complicate the achieving of others? For instance, would the attempt to restrict the speaker's topic interfere with the broader goal of attracting that person to your school or club? If so, which aim is more important? Do you want a particular speaker at any cost or only under certain conditions? Can you think of ways to accommodate all your purposes?

Write down some information, derive some assertions that you think will help achieve each purpose, and come up with a tentative organizing idea for a letter of invitation. Then write a first draft of the letter. When you have completed the draft, ask others to read it, especially your classmates who are writing similar letters. When your readers have commented on how fully the letter serves your purposes, rewrite it, incorporating any suggestions you find helpful. When you have finished your letter, ask yourself the following questions about each paragraph in it, and make further revisions, if necessary, to achieve your objectives.

1. Does each paragraph convey an organizing idea?
2. Does the organizing idea of each paragraph reflect your main purpose?
3. If it fails to reflect your main purpose, how would you revise it?

All writing is purposeful, of course, not just letter writing. Imagine, for example, that you have been asked by the editor of your home-town newspaper to write an essay describing your family's history from the time of your great-grandparents to the present. What purposes might direct your writing in this instance? Certainly, one purpose would be to communicate the relevant facts, names, dates, places, and events that make up your family history. But a mere listing of this information would probably be boring to most readers of your home-town newspaper. Another purpose, therefore, would be to make that history interesting to readers by giving it a slant—perhaps by emphasizing the lives of those relatives who served your home town in politics or education or some other sphere, or by focusing on a particular person whose life or talents or idiosyncrasies might make interesting reading.

Naturally you would have expressive purposes as well in writing this story. Through your manipulation of style, word choice, and tone you might create a humorous or earnest or exciting or emotional atmosphere for the telling of your family history. And you might want to create an impression of yourself, too, as a member of that family. Do you want to appear respectful in your telling? Do you want to appear irreverent? Can you think of other communicative or expressive purposes that might guide your writing?

Once you have decided on your intentions, assess the priorities you want to establish among them. Will it be more important to include all the facts about every member of your family for four generations, or more important to emphasize only the most interesting facts pertaining to one or two distinctive individuals? Do you want to stress the family's contribution to the life of your home town more or less than, say, your grandmother's water-color paintings or your great-grandfather's experiences on a farm in nineteenth-century Europe? Do you want your readers to laugh at the antics of your favorite, eccentric uncle more or less than you want them to appreciate your grandparents' struggle to earn a living during the Depression?

Write down some information, derive some assertions that you think will help achieve your purposes, and discover a tentative organizing idea for your essay. Then write a first draft. When you have completed it, ask your classmates to read it and offer suggestions for improving it. Do their responses as readers match your purposes for writing? That is, did they laugh when you wanted them to? Were they moved where you intended to move them? Do they understand what you believe to be the most important or interesting facts about your family's history? If the answer to one or more of these questions is no, you will want to revise your essay so that it more effectively achieves your purpose. Here again are those questions that can guide you in your revision.

1. Does each paragraph convey an organizing idea?
2. Does the organizing idea of each paragraph reflect your main purpose?
3. If it fails to reflect your main purpose, how would you revise it?

4. The Nature of Evidence

In earlier chapters, we emphasized that an organizing idea is an assertion that you as writer formulate in your own mind. We have also shown that your purpose influences your organizing idea as well as your choice of related assertions. This chapter describes how the process of discovering an organizing idea helps you to turn information into evidence.

How Evidence Differs from Information

As you write, you turn information into evidence. Information about any subject is usually available to the writer in great quantity—in fact, far greater than necessary. **Evidence** is the specific information that you choose to include in your statement to support your organizing idea. (You will see later that you can use different evidence to support the same organizing idea for different readers.) Evidence is anything that helps clarify the organizing idea of a statement.

All evidence is information, but not all information is evidence. Here is an example that will help you see the difference. Suppose you are writing a personal opinion essay about the weather in Minnesota. You prefer warm climates to cold climates. This point of view undoubtedly will influence your response to your subject, "the weather in Minnesota." This response might become a tentative organizing idea:

Minnesota is a difficult place to live in the winter.

Which items in the following list of information can serve as evidence for this tentative organizing idea? As you read the list, cross out the items that would probably not be useful as evidence. This approximates one kind of choice you make as you write—the choice to exclude information that is not relevant.

1. long spells of cold weather, ice, and snow
2. ice-skating, skiing, snowmobiles
3. driving in snow is dangerous
4. Minnesotans have to be tougher than Californians to survive
5. I personally don't like snow
6. Minnesota—located between South Dakota and Wisconsin
7. wind-chill factor—effects of cold more extreme
8. winter temperatures thirty-five degrees below zero
9. snow shoveling—a strenuous task
10. farming state

Here is an assessment of each of these pieces of information:

1. Probable evidence:	This piece of information describes the weather in Minnesota and provides a basis for calling the weather uncomfortable.
2. Not evidence:	These pleasurable activities would take too long to relate to the organizing idea, and they may even contradict it.
3. Probable evidence:	Minnesota has large accumulations of snow, and driving in it is hazardous.
4. Not evidence:	It is not related to the organizing idea and is highly questionable information.
5. Probable evidence:	It explains in part the point of view that has given rise to this particular organizing idea.
6. Not evidence:	Although it is true, this information is too general and would probably take too much time and effort to include.
7. Probable evidence:	This information explains why Minnesota is an uncomfortable place in the winter.
8. Probable evidence:	It proves that Minnesota weather is cold in the winter.
9. Probable evidence:	Snow shoveling takes time and energy.
10. Not evidence:	It neither supports nor clarifies the organizing idea.

The following paragraph illustrates how you might use this evidence to support and clarify your organizing idea:

Minnesota has long spells of cold weather, ice, and snow. The wind-chill factor is acute, and temperatures drop as low as 35 degrees below zero. Freezing weather is bad enough, but the snow that comes with it makes life even more difficult. Although some individuals like a life of continual challenges, such as shoveling large amounts of snow, driving on icy, snow-packed roads, and braving cold weather, I personally prefer less stimulating activities, such as relaxing in the sun.

Another writer with a different attitude would write a different statement about Minnesota's weather. For example, if you like winter sports, your organizing idea might be:

Minnesota has the best winter weather in the country.

In this case, to support your opinion, you would probably select as evidence those winter sports that Minnesota residents characteristically enjoy.

Organizing Idea and Evidence

The processes of discovering an organizing idea and of turning information into evidence are so closely related that they affect each other. This relationship could be described as being *reciprocal* or mutual. Each process determines how the other process proceeds. The more information you collect on a given subject, the more certain you become about the precision of your organizing idea; conversely, the more certain you become about your organizing idea, the better you can turn information into evidence that will support it.

Here is another way of stating the reciprocal relationship. Searching for information assists you in locating your organizing idea; conversely, discovering your organizing idea assists you in turning information into evidence. Discovering an organizing idea also helps you to reject information that does not support it.

The following example illustrates how discovering an organizing idea and selecting evidence affect each other. Suppose you are writing a statement on "the abuse of presidential power." You have a purpose: you want to argue that individuals are fallible and that absolute power should not be placed in the hands of one individual. You usually select information that is consistent with your purpose. You are not yet sure of your organizing idea, nor are you certain that all of your information will be useful later. You list your information in order to establish a focus.

Suppose that the following pieces of information represent your early attempts to gather data:

◇ localizing power in the presidency
◇ localized power and effective government
◇ more advantages in localized power
◇ danger—too much power in single individual
◇ unchecked power: egotistical, tyrannical leader

Although you are just beginning to explore your subject, it is useful to test relationships as you gather information in order to discover your organizing idea. Given your purpose and this limited set of information, you might decide at this time that the following tentative organizing idea summarizes the relationships you want to establish:

> Delegating too much power to one individual may turn a representative government into a dictatorship.

As you read about your subject, however, you gather two more pieces of information:

◇ ample constitutional safeguards against a president's abuse of authority
◇ checks and balances written into the Constitution to allow for the free exercise of presidential authority

Suppose that, after studying this new information and its relationship to the data you gathered earlier, you grow more certain of the organizing idea you wish to communicate and you make the following assertion:

> The president should be allowed enough power to enact policy, provided that the people have the means to check any abuse of that power.

Notice how this organizing idea has evolved from your engagement in the process of relating information. You now have a more precise means of organizing the information you have been gathering.

Each piece of information you have gathered so far supports the tentative organizing idea you have discovered. Your information will become evidence because you can use it to support or develop your organizing idea. Moreover, your evolving organizing idea now serves to guide you as you search for still more evidence.

This organizing idea provides a useful means of assessing any new information you might find. Suppose that, as you continue your search, you gather the following pieces of information:

◇ Congress caters to special interest groups
◇ abuses of public power during the Nixon and Johnson administrations
◇ the need for reducing presidential power

Could any of these new assertions be used as evidence? Clearly, the second piece of information, about abuses of power, and the third piece of information, about the need for reducing presidential power, can be evidence for your statement and should be retained because they support your organizing idea. But the first piece, about congressional priorities, does not directly support what you want to say, and it should, therefore, be set aside. It is information, but at this time, it does not appear to be evidence.

You can tell whether a piece of information is useful as evidence by asking, "Does this information either clarify or support what I want to say?" Suppose that while writing about the abuse of presidential power, you have to decide to use or to discard the following piece of information:

◇ a strong figurehead at the top and the smooth running of government

You might decide that this piece of information supports your organizing idea because it implies that presidential power should be maintained. But what about information pertaining to the election of members of Congress? Does this information directly relate to your organizing idea about presidential power? Eventually, you might be able to establish some relationship—if you have enough time and enough space to state its connections to the organizing idea in your statement. It is more likely that you will reject it as evidence, however, because it is not directly related to what you want to say. In any case, the question "Does this support what I want to say?" will help you to pinpoint the connection between any given piece of information and the organizing idea you are trying to develop.

Potentially, any piece of information related to a subject could be turned into evidence for any given organizing idea. But remember that whatever information you select as evidence must clarify and support your organizing idea. If this connection is not clear, then the information is not evidence.

Some pieces of information make better evidence than others; that is, some pieces support or clarify your organizing idea more efficiently than others. You decide the usefulness of a piece of information as evidence by estimating how much time, effort, or space is required to relate it to your organizing idea. Make this decision by comparing the effort you expend with the benefits you derive. Does the effort exceed the benefit?

Remember these three steps for assessing information as possible evidence:

1. Decide if the piece of information is sufficiently relevant to justify the amount of writing required to relate it to your organizing idea.
2. Reject any information that does not meet this test.
3. When you write your statement, be explicit in connecting this relevant information to your organizing idea.

Summary

Evidence is only the specific information that directly supports or clarifies your organizing idea. There is a reciprocal relationship between the process of turning information into evidence and the process of discovering an organizing idea. As you collect more information on a given subject, you become more certain about your organizing idea. As you become more certain of your organizing idea, you can readily convert pieces of information into evidence.

Applying the Concept: Evidence

You may not realize that much of the information solicited from you on application forms or questionnaires ultimately becomes evidence. When you apply for a job, a credit card, or a bank loan, the person studying your response is using that information to draw some conclusion about you. That person determines whether you qualify for a position or for an extension of credit, and that person's inference is based on the information you present. His or her major concern is whether the information you present is evidence that you qualify for the job or the privileges that you have applied for.

Consider an accident report form, which is available at any police station. An elaborate set of questions and diagrams of streets and intersections on this report form are all designed to get evidence, that is, specific information describing the accident. Such questions as "What was the exact location of your automobile?" and "What was the exact location of the other automobile?" are pertinent. But, more important, these forms often require that you write a series of assertions, stating your interpretation of the accident. The facts that you include in this statement are important. For example, you may have been stopped at a signal light when another car, attempting to pass you, struck your car in the rear. Or the other driver may have run a stop sign. This information can be used as evidence to make your interpretation credible.

Even more important, your statements about an accident to your insurance company help the company to assign blame. In the cases presented above, you would probably be assessed as making little or no contribution to the accident. But if your car was sideswiped, or if your car was moving when it was hit by another car, you could be assessed a share of the blame. Since both the number of accidents you are involved in and the degree of fault determined to be yours can raise your insurance, it is important that you use information as precisely as possible, that is, that you make it evidence for your interpretation.

One way to practice distinguishing evidence from information is to prepare to write a paragraph in which you take a stand on an issue. You will need to furnish evidence to support that stand. Focus on an actual situation which you would like to urge others to change and which merits the time and energy required to carry out your purpose. Suppose that one of the major rivers in your home town is about to be altered in a way that you believe does not serve the public interest. A dam is to be constructed on this river; its purpose will be to generate needed electricity. Your organizing idea might be

> The river is more valuable for recreation than for the generation of electricity.

For this reason, you want to persuade local residents to take action against the building of the dam. Here is a list of information. Study the information and try to decide which pieces are evidence and which are not.

LIST OF INFORMATION	PROBABLE EVIDENCE	NOT EVIDENCE
1. There is a plan to designate this river as part of our national wilderness.		
2. Electricity can be obtained from other sources.		

LIST OF INFORMATION	PROBABLE EVIDENCE	NOT EVIDENCE
3. Opinion among the citizens is divided.		
4. Fishing in the river would be reduced.		
5. Salmon use the river as a route to spawning areas.		
6. The river flows through four states.		
7. You have always been opposed to any alteration of the natural environment.		
8. Petitions are now being collected to oppose the dam.		
9. The river was first seen by settlers in 1759.		
10. The river is less than twenty-five miles from six large cities.		

It will be useful to compare your responses with those of your classmates. To assess your efforts, ask the following question about each piece of evidence: "Does this information clarify or support what I want to say?" Remember that brevity is important here; your readers will probably not spend valuable time attempting to decipher a lengthy, rambling statement.

Here is another task that will help you to select evidence for an organizing idea. Suppose you are applying for a job. One basic task requiring the precise use of information is the preparation of a résumé for your prospective employer. You could, no doubt, list a great deal of information about yourself, but how much of that information would be relevant to the job you seek? What kinds of reassurance about you would your employer want to have? If you have not prepared a résumé, this is a good opportunity to practice selecting the most valuable evidence. If you already have a résumé, reconsider your choice of evidence and bring the résumé up to date. Some information will serve as evidence in your behalf for all types of jobs, but each different job is likely to call for different or additional evidence as well.

Although preparing a résumé is a useful place to begin your preparation for the job market, you need more than a résumé to guarantee that you have presented yourself in the most effective way. A sound letter of application is necessary. The following example will provide some suggestions about how you can draft an application.

Suppose you have wanted to be a journalist for as long as you can remember. You now have the opportunity to become an intern for the local newspaper. This internship will give you the chance to learn on the job. It will also pay you some of the money you need to continue your education.

You know that you want the job—you, therefore, already have a purpose—but you are not sure that you can convince the personnel department of the newspaper that you qualify. You begin to list information that you believe might become evidence for your letter of application. Here is such a list:

◇ high school course in journalism
◇ need the money to continue my education
◇ coeditor of school newspaper
◇ three years of high school English
◇ goal: to become journalist
◇ selected to attend regional workshop in journalism
◇ continuing interest in field
◇ college course in rhetoric
◇ contest winner

After studying this list, you might decide on the following tentative organizing idea:

My education and experience indicate that I am qualified to handle a journalism internship.

This organizing idea can now help you assess the usefulness of the information you have gathered. You can do this by asking: "Does the information either support or clarify my organizing idea?"

Look again at the data you have gathered and try to decide whether that information is evidence, probable evidence, or not evidence. Here are some leading questions that will guide your efforts:

How useful is the information that you had three courses in high school English? If the assignments in these courses included a great deal of expository writing, the information is useful; it could indicate that you now have good writing skills, an important qualification for the position you are applying for. If this is not the case, you might find another way to relate this information to your organizing idea. Or if you cannot do so, you might decide to discard it.

How useful is the information that you are now taking a rhetoric course? If, in that course, your independent project focused on journalism, this information could be useful. You might, for example, be involved in research that will help you determine the characteristics of a good news story or of an editorial. If you cannot make such a statement, however, you may add this information to the previous information, documenting your continuing interest in improving your writing.

What about your need for money to continue your education? Does this information relate to your organizing idea? Does it distinguish you from the many other applicants applying for the position? It probably does not and, therefore, should be discarded.

Continuing this procedure will help you to see the reciprocal relationship between gathering information and turning information into evidence. Discovering an organizing idea helps you to assess information; modifying your information, whenever necessary, helps you to state a more precise organizing idea.

When you have completed your assessment, write a first draft. You can tell whether you have fulfilled the assignment by asking yourself the following questions. The members of your class might also want to use these questions to study one another's drafts and to make useful suggestions about how the writing might be revised.

1. What is the organizing idea of each paragraph?
2. Does the information in each paragraph support or clarify the organizing idea?
3. Is some of the information irrelevant to the organizing idea that you mean to convey?

Review of Part 1

In this section, we will review the major concepts introduced in Part 1. Previous chapters have emphasized how writers express their intentions through the process of discovering connections among items of information, stating those connections as assertions, and interrelating the assertions by means of organizing ideas. You can write what you mean by allowing your sense of purpose to guide your discovery of what to say and where and how to say it.

Earlier chapters have described the two basic activities of writing—assembling bits of information and relating them in assertions that establish their significance. By means of these activities you learn about your subject. Your information can include knowledge stored in your mind or jottings on a scrap of paper or extensive written notes from books or magazines. In whatever form, your collection of information reflects what you regard as relevant to your purpose in writing about a particular subject. What you collect is not the only possible list of information, nor does it exhaust the subject. At different times or on other occasions, you might have very different purposes which would provide you with other perspectives on the subject and therefore other collections of information to work with.

Communicating in writing necessitates your turning information into evidence that supports your organizing idea. The information becomes evidence only after you have discovered your organizing idea and have asserted how that information supports it. You may have to discard some of your information because it does not qualify as evidence. You may also discover that you need additional information to accomplish your purpose. As you find pieces of information and relate them in assertions, you develop your tentative organizing idea. As you grow more certain of that idea, you make increasingly more directed choices about how to support it with evidence.

Some Basic Concepts About Writing

A **subject** is that part of a person's environment on which he or she is focusing attention at any given moment. Writing consists of making assertions about a subject.

The writer's **purpose** is whatever the writer wants to achieve by writing. You usually want some particular response from a reader, in which case you usually have some notion of what your purpose is. But you might also have several goals for any written statement, not all of which are clear to you when you begin. Sometimes you discover them or clarify them by writing. In any case, an awareness of both communicative and expressive purposes helps the writer establish the kinds of relationships that are appropriate in a particular written statement.

An **assertion** joins two or more pieces of information in such a way as to specify their relationship. The simplest form of an assertion in writing is the independent clause, or simple sentence, that is, any statement containing a subject and verb that could stand alone. But some assertions may also contain modifying words or word groups, such as dependent clauses, that imply other, more complex relationships.

An **organizing idea** is an assertion that relates other assertions and conveys their unified significance. It represents your judgment about the relevance of all your information in any paragraph or sequence of paragraphs. It can be stated explicitly in the writing, or it can be implied by the way in which individual assertions refer to some relationship they have in common. If it is implied, a reader should be able to express it in a sentence that summarizes the unified impression of a paragraph.

Evidence is that part of the information about some subject that you decide is relevant to your organizing idea. All evidence is information, but not all information is evidence. Evidence is any information that helps to support, clarify, or develop the organizing idea of a statement.

Understanding these basic concepts of Part 1 is essential to understanding the concepts of later chapters. If you are not certain about what they mean or how they function, you may wish to consult your instructor before going on. As you proceed, focus your attention on what happens when you write. As you gow more familiar with the writing process, you can learn to recognize and use your own writing habits to the best advantage.

The Concepts of Part 1: An Illustration

Suppose a writer's subject happens to be "education and the job market." And suppose the writer's main purpose is to express an earnest belief in the value of higher education despite the fact that a college degree cannot guarantee a high-paying job. The writer believes that a college education is important, not because it promises job security, which in fact it does not, but because it civilizes people and develops their capacities to function effectively in the widest variety of personal, social, and even occupational settings.

The writer has listed the following information:

◊ college degree and the job market
◊ more college graduates than available jobs in business and the professions
◊ baby boom of the late 1940s
◊ reasons for going to college
◊ the value of liberal arts courses
◊ learning a trade
◊ more law school graduates than society can absorb
◊ knowledge is power
◊ basic skills: literacy, problem-solving ability
◊ intellectual and emotional maturity
◊ importance of being well-adjusted
◊ different kinds of rewards from college degree

Thinking about these items of information, the writer evolves a tentative organizing idea that reflects the main purpose for writing and also the possibilities of relationships among the pieces of information. Here is the writer's tentative organizing idea:

Going to college no longer ensures a good job, but it does have other advantages that make it worthwhile.

The following paragraphs develop this tentative organizing idea by using the listed information as evidence to support what the writer wants to say. Notice, however, that all the information is not included. The writer has omitted two items that are not sufficiently related to this organizing idea, "baby boom of the late 1940s" and "knowledge is power." But the paragraphs do include the rest of the information.

People can no longer assume that achieving a college degree guarantees a high-paying business or professional career. Numbers alone make such a guarantee impossible: there are simply many more college graduates today than professional and managerial positions for which they are qualified. In some professions, the law, for example, even an advanced degree does not ensure a future in a lawyer's special field. Every available job attracts dozens of eager candidates, all of whom have the talents and the credentials for employment. Getting the job is often more a matter of luck than of preparation. Why, then, should anyone bother with expensive, time-consuming higher education if there is not a predictable payoff at the end?

Answers to this question depend on what "payoff" means to people. If we assume that the only value of a college education is its implicit promise of a good job, then contemporary employment realities deny the usefulness of higher education. But, if payoff is taken in a larger sense to mean more than merely learning a trade, then a college degree may retain its value. What can one learn from college beyond a job specialty? At the least, a student can learn skills that are relevant to efficient living: verbal and mathematical literacy, problem-solving ability, and the capacities to reason carefully and to communicate with others. Beyond these basic skills, one can achieve intellectual and emotional maturity through exposure to the world of ideas, to different points of view, to alternative values, beliefs, and convictions. Liberal arts courses in particular are helpful in developing this maturity.

The payoff, then, lies in the civility, the personal and social adjustment, that higher education can offer. Being well-adjusted is more important to living than being a computer programmer or an executive. Indeed, it may well distinguish the successful programmer or executive from the unsuccessful one; the deeper advantage of higher learning lies in its potential support for the individual coping with life.

Naturally, the developed organizing idea of this statement is subtler than the tentative organizing idea with which the writer began. It is implicit in the statement and can be summarized this way:

> The deeper value of higher education, its contribution to intellectual and emotional maturity, ensures its continued importance to our society despite the fact that a college degree no longer guarantees employment in one's preferred occupation.

Applying the Concepts: Part 1

One way to improve your understanding of the concepts of Part 1 is to analyze their use in some published writing, such as newspaper editorials or letters to the editor. Ask yourself the following questions about each statement. Does it reveal the purposes for which it was written? Are the writer's purposes evident from a first reading? If so, where has the writer indicated a purpose, and how has the writer done so?

Then ask some additional questions. Does the statement convey an organizing idea explicitly, or does it imply one? If it does neither, could you write an assertion that summarizes the statement? Do the other assertions in the statement provide evidence to support or modify its organizing idea? Which assertions would you delete or change? Why would you change them? How would you change them?

After analyzing some published statements, try composing something that demonstrates your progress as a writer and your new awareness of your own writing habits. Choose a subject that interests you, preferably one you have already thought about and for which you can readily list some information fragments. If you are not sure what you want to write about, here are some suggestions. You may wish to choose a subject related to something that you do well, involving either a mental aptitude or a physical ability, or both. For example, you might write about what it takes to survive in the wilderness or about the joys of creative cooking or about keeping bees or arranging music or painting with oils.

Or you might want to focus on some aspect of your own experience, such as an analysis of an incident that profoundly affected your life or a description of a friend whose personality puzzles you. Perhaps you could generalize from your own experience about food and the effects of eating habits or about surprising occurrences in the life of a commuter. Or you might want to take a stand on some recent social change, such as the effect of television on literacy or women in professional life or energy resources as a predictor of future lifestyles or the sounds of punk rock. Your choice of a subject, especially your interest in it, is important. You can avoid dull, lifeless prose if you are interested enough in your subject to want to explain it by writing about it.

After you have decided on a subject, make a list of some information you believe is relevant. Jot down whatever comes to mind or whatever you may find from your reading or research, knowing that you do not have to use everything you jot down. Choose six or seven pieces of information and make assertions about them. Probably, as you make these assertions, information that you had not previously recalled will occur to you. In other words, making an assertion about a range of information will cause you to remember other information that could be added to it. This process is natural, and you will probably stop and start—including and rejecting information as you continue to write. Sooner or later, you will discover a tentative organizing idea that will then help you develop and order your assertions into a unified statement.

As you plan your writing, you may find it useful to discuss your subject and your preliminary ideas about it with fellow students. Talking and explaining can help you see which attitudes you share with others in your class and which are more personal and subjective. After you have completed a draft, you might decide to show your writing to someone who shares your view of the subject, or you might purposely want to share your writing with someone who does not agree with you. Perhaps you are interested in computers or baseball statistics, whereas the person you plan to share your writing with prefers reading modern poetry or going to art exhibits. In any case, letting others read your writing and then reading theirs in return can make you aware of different ideas and alternative choices that may help you in later composing.

When you are ready to revise, the following questions can guide you in assessing the completeness of your writing. They can also help focus your discussion with others in the class.

1. Is the writer's purpose clear? What appear to be the writer's communicative and expressive goals?
2. Is the organizing idea of the essay explicitly stated or only implied by the assertions the writer makes?

3. Is the organizing idea consistent with the writer's purpose?
4. Does each paragraph have its own organizing idea, which relates the pieces of information in the paragraph?
5. Does the information in the written statement support or clarify the statement's organizing idea? In other words, is it evidence or not?

Part 2: Writing to Readers

5. The Reader's Frame of Reference

Whereas Part 1 focused on the writer's relationship to a subject, the three chapters of Part 2 will focus on the writer's relationship to the intended reader. Earlier chapters explained how writers, with specific purposes in mind, gather useful information about their subjects, generate assertions that clarify relationships among pieces of information, and unify these assertions by means of an organizing idea. The next three chapters will show you how to use a reader's needs to guide you in accomplishing your purposes. Experienced writers try to take into account their reader's point of view or frame of reference, which usually differs from their own.

What Is a Frame of Reference?

A **reader's frame of reference** is a composite of his or her feelings, assumptions, experiences, and values. It is that person's perspective or world view. Because of their different frames of reference, people respond to the same thing in different ways. Personality theorists have discussed the origins of a person's frame of reference, but we will discuss frame of reference only as it affects your writing to a reader.

Consider "the moon" as a subject. To a child, the moon may be a face in the sky; to a poet, a symbol; to an astrologer, a sign governing personality. To a primitive person, the moon may be a deity; to an astronomer, a celestial body moving through space; to spacecraft engineers, a set of mathematical coordinates. Many other responses are possible, each determined by the individual's frame of reference.

The Reader's Role in Your Writing

Any time you write, you have some assertions to communicate to a reader. Your communicating depends on your recognizing that there is a difference between your reader's frame of reference and your own. Communicating also depends on your recognizing that readers have different frames of reference. Consider the following situations:

How would you describe an iceberg to a desert dweller? Would you compare it to a snow-covered mountain, or would you compare it to a large sand dune?

Suppose you wanted to build a new supermarket. Would you tell neighborhood citizens opposed to your plans that a new supermarket is desirable because of its long-term guarantee of profit, or would you speak instead of the convenience of neighborhood shopping? Would you tell a city commissioner in charge of urban development the same things you might tell the neighborhood citizens?

Would you describe the value of the space program to a politician in terms of the theory of space flight, or would you describe it in terms of practical advantages, such as weather forecasts, improved communications, and national defense?

Would you tell fifth graders that both organic and inorganic chemistry are needed in a premed curriculum, or would you tell them that they should study science if they want to be doctors?

The Writer's Contract with the Reader

To communicate clearly in your writing, you will need to consider your reader's frame of reference. In any writing situation, there is an implied contract between the writer and the reader. You promise to tell your reader the significance of your information, hoping that he or she will continue to read. Your reader will continue to read as long as you recognize his or her perspective. If you fail to recognize your reader's perspective, you break the contract, and the reader may stop reading. Whenever you forget your reader's frame of reference, you fail to communicate.

You may not have thought about the reader's difficulty in understanding what you write. Since you are concerned with making assertions about your subject, you may have overlooked your reader entirely. Why bother with the reader's frame of reference? Why not just present the information and let the reader attempt to discover what is significant about it? If you know what you mean, why should your reader be puzzled?

These are common questions. They arise from a false assumption that satisfying yourself also satisfies your reader. These questions presume that your choices do not affect your reader's ability to comprehend and that a reader can understand anything you say, in any way you choose to say it. Writers who make these assumptions feel free to write only approximately what they think they mean, believing that their readers will make the effort to understand it. But they are wrong. No such superhuman reader exists. No reader will make an effort to understand if the writer has not first made an effort to communicate.

Common experience tells you as much. Readers are only human. They will not organize your information for you, and they are not completely flexible in their attitudes or their assumptions. They do not know precisely the same information the writer knows, nor do they see the world in precisely the same way. The writer cannot expect them to. The writer and the reader do not share the same assumptions about their environment, and so they do not respond to it in the same way. Their frames of reference are different.

Every time you write, you begin from a position that is different from your reader's position. Suppose you are carrying a table with two friends. They are facing you and walking backwards, and you are giving directions. Suppose you want them to turn their end of the table to your right. What would you tell them? Their frame of reference is opposite to yours, and their frame of reference is the one that counts. In order to move the table to your right, you must tell them to move the table to their left.

How well you communicate depends on your recognizing that your perspective differs from the perspective of any of your readers, and that their perspectives differ from each other. You have a frame of reference, but so does your reader: you see one organizing idea in a set of information, but your reader is likely to see another. You will make sense to your reader only insofar as you are able to reconcile these differences as you write.

The Effect of Your Reader's Frame of Reference

A comparison of two statements with essentially the same organizing idea, but written to two different readers, will show the difference between two frames of reference and also how that difference affects the writer's choices. Consider the following statements. Notice the selection and organization of information in each statement. See if you can recognize the kind of reader to whom each statement might have been written. Here is a list of possible readers to guide you in reader recognition.

a. a person who feels that auto races are dangerous and not a sport
b. a person who prefers tennis and rarely watches auto races
c. a member of the Indiana State Racing Commission

STATEMENT 1

As a racing enthusiast, I have always accepted the inevitable hazards of the sport. When cars travel at speeds approaching 200 miles per hour, serious accidents will sometimes occur. Drivers are aware of the risk in their profession and are generally willing to accept it, assuming reasonable safety measures. But the large number of fatal accidents in recent years has focused some bad publicity on the sport and made reform an issue of serious importance. The Indianapolis Raceway in particular is an old track no longer suited to the speeds of modern vehicles. I urge you, therefore, to consider design changes in both the track and the cars, thereby ensuring that the tragedies of earlier seasons are not repeated in the future.

STATEMENT 2

I agree that fatal accidents in recent years have focused some bad publicity on the sport of auto racing. To prevent such serious incidents in the future, reform is essential, particularly at the Indianapolis Raceway, which is an old track unsuited to the speeds of modern vehicles. But the inevitable hazards of the sport need not overshadow its entertainment value as long as reasonable safety measures are enforced. Drivers accept the risk involved in traveling at speeds approaching 200 miles per hour and are good enough at their profession to minimize that risk. Design alterations, both in the track at Indy and in the cars that race there, are soon to be implemented. When they are, the excitement of auto racing will be matched by the quality of its safety standards.

To which of the possible readers was each statement addressed? Both statements express essentially the same organizing idea: the writer—in favor of auto racing and concerned about its future—argues for its preservation, at the same time insisting on the need for certain reforms.

To compare the two statements, notice the beginning of each. In statement 1, the writer opens by declaring enthusiasm for auto racing. In statement 2, the writer opens by noting the bad publicity resulting from fatal accidents. What do these beginnings indicate about the intended readers?

In each of these statements, the writer makes strategic choices by anticipating the reader's perspective. It is reasonable to assume that a member of the racing commission might recognize the need for reform but still might eagerly support racing as a sport. If you wish to communicate your view of racing to this reader, would you begin by insisting on its high mortality rate? Such an opening would invite immediate argument and might alienate this reader from the start. A more effective opening would be to express your enthusiasm for racing first and then to propose the need for reform.

Would you use the same strategies for a reader opposed to auto racing that you would use for the racing commissioner? Obviously not. It is more likely that the opponent of racing would fear the hazards of the sport and would need to be convinced about its entertainment value. How well would you communicate to this reader if you began by stating your own enthusiasm for the sport? An opening that asserts enthusiasm would alienate this reader because it would ignore the reader's immediate concerns. A better opening might be to admit the hazards and the need for reform. Later on you could argue for the enjoyment of the sport if safety were ensured.

Statement 1, therefore, is probably aimed at reader c, the racing commissioner, and statement 2 is probably aimed at reader a, the opponent of auto racing. In each case, the reader's perspective has affected the writer's strategy for presenting information. In statement 1, the writer begins with an expression of enthusiasm for auto racing, thereby anticipating the reader's frame of reference. Only after acknowledging the similar perspectives between reader and writer does the writer assert the necessity of reform.

In statement 2, the writer recognizes the intended reader's opposing argument—namely, racing's high death rate—right at the beginning. The writer then concedes the need for reform. Only later, having already anticipated the reader's major objections, does the writer argue for the value of the sport. Each statement, therefore, acknowledges the reader's frame of reference as it conveys the writer's organizing idea.

By using your reader's frame of reference as you write, you can judge the most effective way to communicate your assertions. This strategy can result in other choices for developing paragraphs, but no matter what choices you make, your concern for your reader's perspective will influence your presentation of information.

Focusing on a Reader

When presenting your information, you must anticipate what your reader is capable of understanding or acknowledging. Your task is to state the significance of your information in such a way that your reader can comprehend the assertions you are making. To accomplish this task, you will need to acknowledge your reader's frame of reference. In other words, you must focus on the reader.

To focus on a reader is to anticipate that reader's response. You do this by inferring what feelings, assumptions, experiences, or values will influence that reader's response to your subject. It does not mean that you must compromise your organizing idea merely because your reader might not agree with it. It does mean that you make use of the reader's perspective in order to present your organizing idea in a way that convinces your reader that it has some merit.

Focusing on Different Readers: An Illustration

In each of the two paragraphs below, the writer states a similar idea, namely, that smoking in public should be restricted to specific places. What the writer changes is the way in which the information is presented; the strategies employed reflect the writer's awareness of the reader's frame of reference. From the following list of possible readers, see if you can choose the most probable reader to whom each paragraph might have been written.

a. a college freshman just beginning to smoke

b. a smoker who has smoked for twenty-nine years

c. a nonsmoker

d. the owner of a crowded, popular restaurant

PARAGRAPH 1

Certainly it is difficult to give up an activity that provides many pleasures. Smoking is such a pleasurable activity for many people, who claim that it offers benefits they are not willing to give up, such as a release from tension, a welcome respite from a task, or a way to control one's appetite for food. Recently, however, nonsmokers have become more outspoken about their right to clean air; accordingly, they resent people who, they claim, pollute the air with cigarette smoke. One way to diminish the possible tension that could result from these two radically opposed viewpoints would be to restrict smoking in public to specific places. If such a compromise were achieved, smokers could continue to engage in their habit without having to face the resentment of nonsmokers, and nonsmokers could go about their affairs without worrying about potential damage to their health.

PARAGRAPH 2

Business people whose livelihood depends on pleasing the public are now facing the dilemma of how to please both the smokers and nonsmokers who visit their establishments. Those people who have smoked for most of their lives insist on their right to continue, whereas people who do not smoke resent having to breathe polluted air. One possible solution is to provide a specific place for smokers to congregate, restricting the remaining area to nonsmokers. In this way, both smokers and nonsmokers will feel that their wishes are respected, and both will be less likely to take their business elsewhere.

Despite writing to two very different readers, the writer, probably a nonsmoker, has not compromised his or her position or purpose—to argue for the right to an environment unpolluted by cigarette smoke. In paragraph 1, the writer has addressed the argument to reader b, a smoker who has smoked for twenty-nine years. The writer not only has respected that reader's perspective but also has indicated that smokers will benefit from the proposed compromise, since they will thereby avoid the resentment of nonsmokers. In paragraph 2, the writer has taken into consideration the perspective of reader d, the owner of a crowded restaurant, arguing for the proposed compromise while further pointing out to that reader the means of avoiding any possible loss of business.

Through this process of considering the viewpoint of intended readers, writers gain a benefit for themselves, an enlarged view of their subjects. They come to see those subjects from a less subjective frame of reference, and the result is a richer perception of what they want to say. Focusing on a reader's needs, therefore, is a way to learn as well as a way to communicate.

Summary

You learn about your subject by explaining the significance of your information to your intended reader. You explain this significance by first anticipating your reader's response to your organizing idea. That is, you focus on your reader, inferring what feelings, assumptions, experiences, or values will influence that reader's response to your subject.

Applying the Concept: The Reader's Frame of Reference

A useful way to understand the notion of focusing on a reader is to study various types of writing that are obvious attempts to communicate to readers. You have probably received brochures through the mail that attempt to persuade you to act in a certain manner. Typical are the mailing pieces from special interest groups: a request for money to support a worthwhile cause, a campaign statement from a political candidate, a form letter from your senator, or a plea from a neighborhood group of citizens for your support in preventing a change in zoning. Such pleas are common; they are easy to find. You and the members of your class might collect a dozen or more of these mailing pieces. Look for appeals that represent various special interest groups; they all have a cause, and they all solicit your help. Here are some examples of such mailing pieces:

◊ a request from a citizen group that you support its attempts to persuade politicians of the need for handgun control
◊ a request from a lobby that you support its efforts in behalf of solar energy rather than nuclear energy
◊ an appeal for funds to support an international organization, such as the Red Cross or the USO
◊ an invitation to join an organization concerned with the federal funding of social programs

Once you have gathered these reader-oriented pieces of prose, ask yourself the following questions about each. Does the request document the goals and achievements of the cause or organization? Does it acknowledge the reader's frame of reference? Does it clarify the benefits a reader will receive by complying with the requests?

You might also want to study some advertisements of services and decide how well these advertisements address readers. For example, if a local group of college students offer their services—window washing, gardening, heavy and light cleaning—to raise money to support the tutoring of underpriviledged children, what benefits would you expect the advertisement to emphasize? Look at different kinds of advertisements. What appeal would a tobacco advertisement attempt to establish? What would the advertisement for a bank have in common with the advertisement for a food store or a clothing shop or a drugstore? Studying advertisements will help you analyze all the various promotional literature that you collect.

Then study all these promotional pieces again. Ask yourself how each statement focuses on the reader and accommodates the reader's needs or wants. How does each statement relate the writer's purpose to the reader's needs? Does it represent some kind of experience with which readers can presumably identify themselves? Has the writer tried to convince the reader that taking action will either rescue the reader from an undesirable situation or result in a desirable one? Next, you might want to consider whether the statement manages to convey the writer's purpose, even while addressing the reader. Has the writer defeated his or her purpose by focusing too narrowly or too intensely on the reader's needs?

Finally, you might want to suppose a different readership. Could the statement have conveyed this purpose in exactly the same way to someone with a totally different frame of reference? What kind of reader, for example, would be persuaded by some of the current advertisements of jeans for women? What kind of reader would respond to the question, "Are you sickened by the violent use of handguns?" These are useful questions when applying the concepts presented in this chapter.

Once you have studied models of reader-oriented prose, you may wish to make your own statement. A useful way to strengthen your ability to express yourself by accommodating the reader is to choose a topic you feel strongly about and then to write two statements to readers who differ from each other in the way they view your subject. Have you recently been annoyed at some inconvenience or embarrassment? Is your dorm room unsuited to your needs? Is your roommate difficult to live with? Are the computer printouts of your tuition bill or your class schedule inaccurate? Has your teacher given you a grade you disagree with? Has a check of yours bounced because of a bank error?

You might choose, however, to explore some larger issue about which you feel strongly. You might consider such issues as the appropriate treatment for people who shoot public leaders or the failure of

American democracy because too great a division exists between the haves and have-nots, the educated and uneducated, the skilled and unskilled.

How about exploring a matter that perplexes you? For example, do neglectful parents have a right to their children? Do children in wealthy communities deserve the right to a better education than children in poorer communities. Have the goals of American workers changed? Are they now as concerned with the satisfaction of their own psychological needs as they are with the need for adequate income?

These subjects are all broad enough to invite many different kinds of responses from readers. Consider writing twice about some such subject, once to each of two different readers. One reader might be a trusted friend or adult who will automatically be sympathetic to your frame of reference; the other might be a person who is unknown to you, someone in an official capacity, a person who might be able to help you or to take action if approached sensibly. Can you convey your organizing idea in a way that indicates your sensitivity to other frames of reference?

Once you have an organizing idea, you might want to discuss with others in your class the readers you have chosen and your hunches about their different frames of reference. Ask your classmates how they think different readers might respond. A friend, for example, might have shared your experience and would therefore be sympathetic to your view. A housing office director or a clerk in a comptroller's office or a bank manager or a politician or the director of a company might have questions that might not be so easily dealt with. For example, the housing director may want to know why your room should be changed or how unbearable your situation really is; the clerk might need more explanation from you before being able to address your grievance about your tuition bill or your class schedule; the politician may want to know how representative your opinion is; and the director of a company may wonder what effect addressing psychological needs has on productivity. Considering their questions will enlarge your sense of your subject and thereby lead to a shrewder assessment of what you can say.

You and the members of your class may decide to work together, reading each other's drafts according to the following criteria:

1. Does the writing sample focus on the reader's frame of reference?
2. Does the evidence used in the writing sample address the reader's perspective?
3. Does the writer consistently maintain a purpose or purposes?

6. Writing to Your Intended Reader

In Chapter 5, we emphasized the concept of a reader's frame of reference, which we described as a composite of a person's feelings, assumptions, experiences, and values. One's frame of reference is a perspective that is unique to each person, so your reader's frame of reference differs from yours and also from the perspectives of other readers. In order to communicate to a reader, you will need to identify that reader's frame of reference to some degree so that it can guide the way you present your information. Chapter 5 showed you how the same set of information could be developed differently for different frames of reference.

In this chapter, we will explain how you can use your reader's frame of reference to guide you in formulating your organizing idea. That frame of reference can also help you to develop your organizing idea after you have started to compose your statement.

You can use your reader's frame of reference by thinking of the most important question your reader might ask you. This chapter will show you how to consider that question even when you do not know who your reader is or when you are writing to many different readers at once.

The Reader's Implied Question

The **reader's implied question** represents the reader's attempt to relate the writer's organizing idea to his or her own perspective. This implied question is essentially "What will this statement mean to me?" There are many versions of this question: What is the significance of what you are telling me? How will it affect me? What are its consequences? Why should I pay attention to it? But they all seek the same information. Specifically, your readers need to know how your organizing idea will apply to their unique frames of reference.

The reader's implied question is not a matter of agreement or disagreement between the writer and the reader; it is a matter of relevance. You can reasonably assume at least some interest on the part of the reader in the subject about which you are writing; otherwise, you would not be trying to communicate. But given that interest on the reader's part, however weak or intense it might be at the start, your reader needs to estimate the significance of what you are likely to say about the subject. Can you present your subject in a way that makes it possible for the reader to cope with the information that you want to convey?

Suppose, for example, that your broad subject is "nutrition." How would you narrow it if your readers were a group of eighth-grade students? Would you discuss in detail the hazards of chemical substitutes as you might to a college student majoring in nutrition? Would you outline a balanced diet as you might to a person who is responsible for planning family meals? Probably not. You would choose information by keeping in mind an eighth grader's frame of reference. In each case, your listener or reader brings a different perspective to your subject. Communicating depends on your focusing your organizing idea on the implied question derived from a reader's perspective.

Consider the following situation. As part of your half-time work for an ecology center, you are currently researching a paper that focuses on the environment and the automobile. You have concluded from information drawn from several major studies that automobiles are a major source of environmental pollution. You want to explain your work at the center to two people who are interested in your activities: one is your mother or father; the other is an adult relative, say, an uncle. Your parent drives a small car, remains within the speed limit, and participates in a car pool. Your uncle drives a large car, does not respect the posted speed limit, and views car pools as an intrusion on his precious time. Would you address both of these readers in the same way? Obviously not, because their frames of reference are different. But it is easier and faster to organize your information in each case when you consider each reader's perspective in terms of the same implied question: "Why should I be interested in the research you are doing?"

What response can you anticipate from each person? Both have reasons for their driving habits. Your parent's opinion might be that he or she likes small cars, prefers to drive at a reasonable speed because it is safer, and dislikes driving any more than is absolutely necessary. Your uncle's opinion might be that small cars are dangerous because the driver is more likely to be hurt in an accident, that speeding is sometimes necessary considering the rapid pace of life, and that he can use the time driving alone to think or to plan other activities. If you can anticipate some version of the question these readers may ask, you will be able to express your ideas while taking into account each reader's unique perspective.

Do not feel that you need to compromise your purpose or your organizing idea just because your reader may disagree with it. Nor should you try to manipulate the reader by pretending that your perspectives are identical. Instead, you can present your organizing idea in a way that enables each intended reader to understand it more readily and to be more receptive to it.

By acknowledging the reader's implied question, you can gain two benefits. One benefit is that you will keep the reader interested; the other is that you will simplify your own task. It is easier and faster to organize for someone else than it is to organize for yourself. It is easier and faster to discover what you want to say when you let your reader's frame of reference guide you in selecting and arranging information. If you can anticipate your reader's implied question, your choices are already directed toward some kinds of information and away from others. Since you can select many things to say about any subject, you can use your reader to guide and limit your choices. If you think in terms of what your reader needs to know, you can save time and effort deciding what you want to say.

Writing to an Intended Reader: An Illustration

Assume you are writing to two different readers about the rights of women. Your two readers' frames of reference are different, but your organizing idea is the same: "There should be a steady movement toward equality for women, but complete equality cannot be achieved all at once." You have selected the following information for your statements:

1. equal pay for equal work
2. men and women should enjoy equal status within families

3. militancy is dangerous and ineffectual
4. a question of consciousness raising
5. protests and demonstrations only cause aggravation

Your first reader is a male business executive. You understand that this executive prefers peace and tranquility to social chaos, whatever the merits of the cause. This preference constitutes part of his frame of reference. He firmly believes that the women's movement is composed of noisy, disruptive women who have created more problems than they have solved. He might ask, "Where is all this social turmoil leading us?" Or he might ask, more specifically, "What inconvenience will the women's movement cost me?" You might consider either of these to be this reader's implied question. Or you might anticipate some other questions.

The following statement illustrates one way to present your organizing idea to this reader. In this case, you might acknowledge the reader's frame of reference by first presenting information that the reader is already disposed to accept. Then you might argue the case by consistently acknowledging this reader's perspective, but without compromising your organizing idea. Here is how such a paragraph might develop:

> The disruptive protests of the more militant women's groups have caused irritation to many people during the past fifteen years. But this irritation should not blind us to the fact that these groups have a good deal to complain about. For example, industry has always prided itself on judging a person solely on the basis of performance, but it has traditionally paid women less and promoted them more slowly than their male counterparts. We can't have complete equality tomorrow; more consciousness raising among both men and women must take place before that occurs. But a steady movement toward male-female equality in business and social relations must continue. Otherwise, by denying half the population the rights supposedly guaranteed to all, we justify the protests.

If you attack your reader's assumptions, your reader will probably reject your organizing idea. On the other hand, you can acknowledge your reader's assumptions and then use those assumptions to introduce what you want to say: "Granted the protests are disruptive, yet they have some justification"; "granted some progress has been made, but there is much yet to be done"; "granted we cannot afford immediate equality at the cost of drastic social upheaval, but we are obligated to guarantee equal rights to all men and women."

Now for the second reader. Suppose this reader is a law student. The reader's opinion is that equality between men and women must be constitutionally protected—at once, in all areas, at all costs. His implied question might be something like this: "How do we get started?" or "What must be done to enable these changes to occur?"

Should you approach this reader as you did the business executive? Will your writing strategies be the same? Here is a paragraph that anticipates the frame of reference of your second reader; notice how it differs from the first paragraph in the way it acknowledges the reader's assumptions about "the need for equality."

> The subordinate place of women in the past justifies the current drive for equal rights. But disruptive tactics, which create resentment rather than understanding, do not aid this effort. Five thousand years of social history cannot be changed in a single generation. Men and women should receive equal pay, and they should have equal family responsibilities. Any attempt to legislate immediate equality in all fields will lead to resentment among men and women. Accordingly, traditionalists will avoid compliance. The way to achieve sexual equality is through education, the raising of men's social consciousness as well as women's. The key to equality is education rather than demonstrations.

Identifying the Unknown Reader

Writing to an unknown reader is a situation that news and magazine writers, for example, confront every day. These writers direct their statements not to an individual person but to a typical reader, who has a set of traits or characteristics that they believe most of their readers share. In other words, these writers focus on traits that most of their readers have in common. Every newspaper and magazine assumes a typical reader and focuses on the traits of that reader. Are you familiar, for example, with the traits of the people who read *Cosmopolitan* or of those who read *Argosy*? If not, you could infer at least some of the traits of each group of readers by scanning the advertising pages and the table of contents of each magazine. You might find some similarities among the traits of each group of readers, and you would certainly find some differences.

Similarly, the intended reader of *Family Circle* is obviously different from the intended reader of *House Beautiful.* The intended reader of *Time* is different from the intended reader of *U.S. News and World Report.* One can readily estimate a reader's approximate age, knowledge of a given subject, political affiliation, social class, annual income, moral values, personal interests, and other characteristics as well. Writers for these publications select and organize their information, keeping in mind the characteristics that their readers share, although the writers do not know the individuals who are going to buy the newspaper or magazine.

The Characteristics of the Common Reader

Whenever you are uncertain of the individual who might be your reader, you can take advantage of a construct called the common reader, just as journalists do. Writing to a common reader is often preferable to addressing an individual because the common reader's frame of reference is more easily recognizable than that of any individual. Although you might often be mistaken or unsure about the unique and continually changing frame of reference of a given individual, the characteristics of a common reader are constant. If you focus on these characteristics, you will find that the common reader can be your most reliable guide in many writing situations.

The **common reader** is a model that you construct in your mind, an all-purpose reader that you create on the basis of characteristics that all readers share. In order to use the concept of the common reader, you must first recognize these characteristics. The most important is the reader's *ignorance of your organizing idea.* The common reader may know a great deal about your subject in general, but the common reader does not know your organizing idea. In other words, no reader knows your organizing idea before you convey it. You can assume that your reader needs all the guidance you can give about how you are developing your organizing idea.

The second major characteristic of the common reader is *impatience.* The common reader wants you to get to the point. Whatever you are going to say will modify the reader's understanding of your subject, and naturally the reader is impatient to find out the significance of your organizing idea.

The common reader, then, is a construct that you build in your mind based on what is true of all readers, namely, their ignorance of your organizing idea and their impatience. These two traits are what make the concept of the common reader so reliable. You can use them no matter whom you address.

In addition to these two major characteristics, there are three secondary characteristics that are useful. If you wish, you can make three further assumptions about the common reader. Assume that the common reader is like you in these respects: the reader has reached the *same level of maturity* that you have reached, has achieved about the *same level of formal education* that you have achieved, and *knows approximately as much as you do about your subject*. This third characteristic should not mislead you. Knowing your subject is not the same as knowing your organizing idea. The common reader could know a fair amount about your subject without even being aware of your organizing idea.

You might ask: "Why these three secondary characteristics and not others?" The answer is that addressing these characteristics will help you sound more like yourself. You are already familiar with frames of reference that are typical of your own level of maturity, your own level of education, and your own knowledge of the subject. If you focus on these three secondary traits in the common reader, your writing will sound more natural.

Notice a crucial distinction here: the distinction is between writing merely to yourself, which denies communication, and writing to someone else because your purpose is to communicate. The construct of the common reader is a convenient way for you to identify your reader; it helps you to write to others, but in a way that feels natural. If you happen to have specific information about your reader, then use it; if not, then the frame of reference represented by your common reader will be a useful guide in whatever you write.

Summary

In order to engage your reader in what you are writing, you will need to acknowledge that reader's frame of reference, whatever it might be. One way to acknowledge it, given whatever you know about that reader, is to imagine what his or her most urgent question is likely to be about your organizing idea. Even guessing at this question will help you to formulate your statement. If you know very little about your reader, or if you are addressing many different readers at once, you can use the notion of the common reader, which will furnish you with a dependable frame of reference for formulating your organizing idea.

Applying the Concept: Writing to Your Intended Reader

As we have suggested, focusing on an intended reader—whether a known reader or the common reader—yields two benefits to the writer. The more obvious benefit is that you can keep your reader interested. Various strategies can help you capture this interest. You can say at the start that you are aware of your reader's opposing attitude and later indicate that differences between your attitude and your reader's are not as great as they appear. Or you might focus at first on shared assumptions, revealing later how your stand differs from your reader's.

The other benefit of focusing on your intended reader—and probably the primary benefit—is that you thereby narrow the kind of information that you can profitably use in your statement. Consider the following questions, for example, which illustrate how focusing on a reader necessarily narrows the range of information pertaining to your subject:

> What kinds of information would you select to tell an eighth grader about a famous novelist? (List four or five pieces of appropriate data.)

> What kinds of information about the novelist would you select to tell a person who wants a few relaxing books for summer reading? (List four or five pieces of appropriate data.)

> What kinds of information about this novelist would you select to tell a graduate student who is studying the novel as an art form? (List four or five pieces of appropriate data.)

Some of the information you have listed may be appropriate to all three groups of readers; some may not. What pieces of information appropriate to one group of readers would not interest either or both of the other groups?

To understand the benefits to be gained from thinking about your reader's implied question, you might gather some magazine articles that address different audiences. Try to find articles on the same subject but written from varying points of view, perhaps a controversial subject such as the legal voting or drinking age, the ratification of the ERA, or tax or welfare reform. How does the writer focus on the reader? Which assertions seem most likely to capture the intended reader's interest? How useful would any of these assertions be in any of the other statements that you have collected?

If you cannot name the intended readers for any of these statements, the common reader will do. As you may recall, two traits are shared by all readers: ignorance of your organizing idea and impatience to know what it is. Has the writer paid attention to these two traits? Has the writer avoided a patronizing or elitist tone by recognizing the three secondary traits of the common reader? Does the writer assume that the reader knows as much about the subject as the writer does? Does the writer assume that the reader is approximately the writer's age and has received a comparable education?

After you have determined the strategy that each writer has used in addressing readers, scan the different statements until you have a good sense of the information they contain. Can you explain why each writer restricted his or her information? Given all the information in any one of the statements, did the writer make shrewd choices? Which items of information in one statement might serve another statement? Which might not?

To apply the concepts described in this chapter to your own writing, think about a subject that interests you and that might invite various responses from readers. Then jot down a list of information about it for each of several different readers. Here are some suggestions for topics and for potential readers.

SUBJECT 1:   NUTRITION
Reader 1:   Your uncle who is convinced that the current concern with good nutrition is a fad, encouraged by business people who profit from overpriced "health foods"
Reader 2:   Your roommate who describes himself or herself as a "junk food addict"
Reader 3:   Your boy friend or girl friend who knows little, if anything, about your subject
Reader 4:   Your mother who is concerned about what you eat

SUBJECT 2:   MEDITATION
Reader 1:   Your best friend's father who is convinced that meditators are merely lazy people who use meditation as a rationalization for their lack of productivity

Reader 2:	Your best friend's mother who is afraid her daughter or son may become a college dropout because of an interest in meditation
Reader 3:	A tense friend who drinks or smokes in order to relax
Reader 4:	A news writer who suspects that meditation might limit productivity

SUBJECT 3:	JOGGING
Reader 1:	A sedentary adult who is in poor shape
Reader 2:	A hypochondriac who is afraid that intense physical exercise is detrimental to one's health
Reader 3:	A friend who pulled the ligaments in her knee while jogging and had to walk on crutches
Reader 4:	A person who sneers at the jogging craze, believing it is fostered by those who profit from jogging attire

SUBJECT 4:	COMPUTER RECORDS AND PRIVACY
Reader 1:	A computer salesperson who argues for the efficiency of computerized storage of records
Reader 2:	A man whose computerized health insurance records were accidentally sent to his employer
Reader 3:	An intelligent woman who is concerned about possible infringements on her right to privacy
Reader 4:	The common reader

SUBJECT 5:	FEDERAL BUDGET CUTS AND SOCIAL PROGRAMS
Reader 1:	A young parent who works at two jobs in order to support a family
Reader 2:	A college student who depends on student loans to continue her education
Reader 3:	A person who has benefited greatly from a social program now being dropped
Reader 4:	The common reader

Use these suggestions if they interest you, but, if they do not, feel free to select your own subject and choose your own reader.

Once you have chosen a subject and identified the reader, you are ready to decide what you want to assert about your topic. You may want to recall the guidelines established in Part 1; they will help you clarify your purpose and formulate a tentative organizing idea. It is important to establish at least a tentative organizing idea early in your planning, so that you will not compromise what you believe is significant about your subject.

Then focus on your intended reader and ask yourself these questions: What is that reader's frame of reference? How might that reader view your subject? How might you take into account that reader's perspective without compromising your own organizing idea? Answering these questions will help you to formulate your statement. It is not always easy to accommodate a reader's needs: you may have to compose several drafts and to revise extensively before you are satisfied with your writing.

Whether you use the subjects and readers suggested in this chapter or devise your own, you will probably find it useful to discuss your decisions with members of your class. Together you can decide which assertions appear to be useful, and which do not. As collaborators, you may also want to discuss the reader or readers you have selected and derive the implied question that each reader might ask. You might want to take turns playing the roles of different intended readers. How would *you* respond to a given statement if you were its expected audience? Or you could read your classmates' drafts with a view to helping them better anticipate their readers' needs. Addressing the following questions to their texts—as well as to your own—will help you judge the effectiveness of the draft:

1. Does the statement acknowledge the reader's frame of reference, or does it merely state an organizing idea?
2. If the intended reader is the common reader, does the sample accommodate all five traits?
3. Has the tentative organizing idea evolved into a developed organizing idea? Or has it been compromised by an appeal to the reader?

7. Evidence for the Reader

Evidence was defined in Chapter 4 as any piece of information that clarifies and supports your organizing idea. There is another factor to consider in selecting evidence: the information must not only support your organizing idea, but it must also be presented in a way that takes into account your reader's perspective or frame of reference. The way to choose evidence by accommodating your reader's frame of reference is the subject of this chapter.

The Usefulness of Functional Evidence

You can determine the best evidence to use in a given writing situation by considering the kinds of information your intended reader needs to know in order to understand your organizing idea. You have seen in Chapters 5 and 6 that focusing on your reader helps you to discover and organize what you want to say. Although you do not change your organizing idea in addressing different readers, you often change or rearrange the evidence you use. The reader you have in mind directly affects the choices you make about what to include and what to omit.

The definition of evidence in Chapter 4 can now be expanded to include what you know about readers. The best evidence is the set of information that most clearly and effectively conveys your organizing idea to your intended reader. We will call such evidence **functional evidence;** it is evidence that you select and arrange specifically for your intended reader.

Some pieces of information are more useful than others as evidence because they support your organizing idea in terms of your reader's frame of reference. Other pieces of information may not be useful to you—even though they could be related to what you want to say—because they do not focus on your reader's perspective. They would not be useful, for example, if they were too obvious, given the reader's knowledge of the subject, or if they were too confusing, given the reader's frame of reference.

Consider the following set of information related to the subject "the basic components of language." Which items do you think an average eighth grader would understand? Put a check opposite those items as you read.

1. The term *morpheme* has become almost meaningless as a label of speech components.
2. Phonetic transcriptions of speech tend to differ from one transcriber to the next and are not always reliable guides to the speech act.
3. Language is often described in terms of sounds, words, and word combinations.
4. The so-called parts of speech are derived from Latin grammar and are not especially helpful in describing English syntax.
5. The parts of speech are noun, pronoun, verb, adverb, adjective, conjunction, preposition, and interjection.
6. Acoustical phonetics is generally supposed to provide more reliable and detailed information about speech than articulatory phonetics.
7. People who study the components of speech are called linguists.

Suppose you were writing about "the components of speech" for two different age groups. Suppose you were writing one statement to students in the eighth grade and another statement to college students specializing in linguistics. All the items in the list could be related to your subject or to an organizing idea concerning "the components of speech." But are all of them useful as evidence if your reader is an eighth grader? (How many did you check on the list above?) Look at the list again. Do your choices remain the same if you are writing to a group of college linguistics majors?

Items 1, about the morpheme, 2, about phonetic transcriptions, and 6, about acoustical phonetics, might be of interest to college students but would be too complex for most younger students.

Item 3, which describes the speech act in a general way, would be useful for the younger student, but it would be useless information in a statement to a student of linguistics (since *word* is not defined in the same way by linguists).

Item 7, which defines linguistics, might be appropriate information for a young student, but it would not be appropriate for a linguistics major.

Every item in this list requires the same kind of decision. Choices about functional evidence in these two writing situations result from the recognition that the perspectives of these two intended readers are different. In any writing situation, the information you choose as evidence for your statement must be evaluated in terms of its relevance both to your organizing idea and to your reader's frame of reference. These two criteria, taken together, will help you select functional evidence.

Finding Functional Evidence: An Illustration

Many people face the familiar task of writing a letter of recommendation for a person who is applying for a job. In this case, the writer's self-evident purpose is to persuade the reader that the candidate is worthy of consideration and that the recommendation is honest, fair, and objective. Specifically, the task is to choose the best—the most compelling—evidence to support the candidate in a way that will convince the reader.

Here is a situation that could entail your writing a letter of recommendation. One kind of employment favored by recent graduates from college is public service in foreign countries. Among the several different federal or philanthropic agencies that hire candidates for such service, the Peace Corps is probably the most familiar.

Suppose a friend of yours is applying for an appointment to the Peace Corps, which is an American service organization helping local communities in many underdeveloped countries of the world. The Peace Corps employs workers who are willing to live overseas and to use their various skills to help others for modest salaries. Although backgrounds in such fields as language, engineering, education, and health care are desirable, the corps needs workers who are willing to learn new skills on the job.

The friend you are recommending must be willing to undergo intensive training and accept low pay in return for working with persons in rural areas of some underdeveloped country. As you are planning your letter, think of a real person; do not invent one.

Who is going to read this letter? Certainly "the Peace Corps" is not going to read it: the Peace Corps is an institution, not a reader. Similarly, you cannot write effectively to a corporation or a bank or a university or a church or a hotel: they are not readers either. Readers are individuals who are affected by what you write and who judge from their own frames of reference how effectively you have presented your information. A bank does not act on your request for a loan, but a reader of loan applications does. A corporation does not consider your request for a raise, but a department head does.

The person who is going to read your letter is a reader of applications to the Peace Corps. Your knowing this reader's job helps you to determine his or her perspective. You can assume that the reader knows what to look for in a Peace Corps candidate, what personality traits are more or less desirable, what kinds of training and job skills are helpful, and where they can most usefully be applied. At the same time, the reader examines hundreds of letters of recommendation from writers like you about individuals like your friend. She or he must make decisions in terms of what you communicate.

Given this reader's perspective, your job is to select functional evidence for a letter of recommendation to the Peace Corps. What kinds of information would you select? Your purpose is to distinguish your friend from all other applicants and to focus the reader's attention on the strengths of this individual. To begin, you can write several possible pieces of information on a sheet of paper. Then apply the following questions to each piece in order to assess its usefulness in helping you accomplish your purpose.

1. Does any piece of information say how long you have known your friend, how well, or under what circumstances—school, work, neighborhood, military service, church, or bowling league? This information could be helpful to a Peace Corps reader. It would reveal how valid your information is likely to be. If you know your friend very well, this information will bear more weight than if you were brief acquaintances.

2. Have you listed any pieces of information that describe what the Peace Corps is about or the nature of its work? Your reader probably knows more about the Peace Corps than you do, so this information is useless.

3. Does any piece of information include your personal assessment of your friend's ability to do Peace Corps work? This information is practically useless. It is up to the reader to decide whether your

friend can do Peace Corps work. It is presumptuous of you to make this decision when you do not know the criteria the reader uses.

4. Does any piece of information include either your personal assessment of the country in which your friend could be placed effectively or what kind of job would be most suitable? This information is equally presumptuous. The Peace Corps reader will decide about such matters. It is your responsibility simply to give information that will help the reader to evaluate your friend.

5. Are there any pieces of information related to your friend's personality traits? This information might be helpful, depending on how your present it. (See items 6, 7, and 8.)

6. If you have listed personality traits, such as "good," "kind," "enterprising," "hard working," "reliable," "likes children and pets," have you provided a telling example or illustration of each one? Details, examples, and specific instances are essential. If you describe your friend merely as "generous," "benevolent," or "humanitarian," you are not helping your reader, for he or she has hundreds of recommendations to look at. If all of them catalogue abstractions, how can the reader distinguish one applicant from another?

7. If you have listed personality traits, how many of them are described in terms of your personal knowledge of your friend? This information reinforces your statement of how long and how well you have known your friend as described in item 1. You must demonstrate firsthand knowledge of your friend's personality and behavior; otherwise, your reader may have some reservation about what you say.

8. Is any piece of information related to your friend's job skills, education, language abilities, specialized training, or experience? This information is obviously useful, depending on how you present it and how detailed you make it.

9. If you have listed special skills, how many of them are detailed in terms of your knowledge of your friend? What foreign language does your friend speak? What job experience did your friend have and for how long? Again, detail is essential. The more specific your description of your friend, the more reliable it becomes for the reader of your statement.

With this evaluation of your information in mind, decide what to include and what to exclude. Then try writing several paragraphs to the Peace Corps reader, using your most effective evidence to recommend your friend. Remember to organize your functional evidence to support your organizing idea. You can do this by acknowledging your reader's implied question about your friend's candidacy—and about your own credibility in describing your friend.

Summary

There are various ways to acknowledge your reader's implied question, even if you cannot answer it fully. Trying honestly to acknowledge this question will make you more credible to your reader. Recognizing your reader's frame of reference helps you to select functional evidence for communicating with that reader. The best evidence for any statement clarifies and supports your organizing idea and accommodates your reader's frame of reference.

Applying the Concept: Functional Evidence for the Reader

Analyzing passages that incorporate functional evidence may help you to use effective evidence in your own writing. In any library, look at two textbooks on the same subject that were written for readers of different ages. Does each book have an organizing idea? Does each include information that supports this organizing idea? And do its assertions connect this evidence in a way that acknowledges a reader's frame of reference? In other words, does each textbook make use of the available evidence to accomplish its purpose? Now consider the ways in which each textbook differs from the other.

Try writing a statement of your own, using functional evidence. Suppose that you want to transfer to another college, seek a summer-abroad scholarship, or request permission to take a special course. Try to choose a writing task that you expect to engage in at some time during your academic career. Creating a fiction or making up false credentials will not help you discover how to represent yourself or how to solve this writing task.

Once you have decided on your task, consider your purpose and state a tentative organizing idea that will explain it, especially in terms that your reader can relate to. For example, if you are writing to some college to request acceptance as a transfer student, you will want to offer a convincing explanation for your request. Your planning and your rough drafts will help you establish such a rationale. Although you may believe that you want to transfer to another institution because you are bored where you are, such information is not sufficiently useful to the admissions officer who must make a decision about your request. What do you mean by the term *bored*? Translate the term *bored* for your reader. Do you mean, for example, that the college you are currently attending will not prepare you to meet your career goals and that the college to which you wish to transfer will prepare you? If that is what you mean, then saying so explicitly will be useful to your reader.

If you are requesting the privilege of taking a course that requires permission, tell the instructor as specifically as you can how this course fits into your overall plans, even if those plans are not yet totally clear to you. If you are requesting a leave of absence, it will help your case if you indicate what your alternative plans will be, how those plans will help you to meet your goals, and, wherever possible, how your goals might be compatible with those of your reader. Let the reader see the detailed reasons for your request, especially if they are compatible with the aims of the institution that the reader represents.

You may recall our proposing in Chapter 4 that you analyze some information we presented as possible evidence for a letter of application. Now is a good time to continue with and extend that activity. These days, with a tight labor market, career counselors generally encourage you to distinguish your employment dossier in some way, and an effective letter of application can serve that end. Your purpose in a job application letter is to advance yourself to the next stage of your negotiation, which is usually an interview. In other words, your purpose in writing is to make your reader want to meet you. But you will probably not succeed in this purpose if you merely indicate that you want the available position and then list all your achievements. Your reader will be impressed with these achievements only if they serve the company's goals, but your reader may not automatically make the connection between your achievements and those goals. What is the connection between the position you want and your field of education, your awards, your job experience, or your future plans? If you do not make these connections, chances are that your reader will not make them either.

To determine whether or not the information you have used in your letter is functional evidence, you might want to share your early ideas and your first drafts with your instructor and classmates. They can help you determine how credible your letter is and how well your request is stated. They can also help you discover some questions your reader might raise. Such interaction will help you to revise deliberately, accommodating your purpose to the needs of your reader.

While you are writing your letter, the following questions will help you assess its quality:

1. Does the evidence in the statement clearly and effectively convey the organizing idea?
2. Does the evidence in the statement clearly and effectively acknowledge the reader's frame of reference?
3. Does the evidence in the statement clearly and effectively acknowledge that reader's implied question?

Review of Part 2

This section reviews the concepts you worked with in Part 2—focusing on an intended reader or on the common reader, anticipating your reader's implied question, and presenting functional evidence. **Focusing on an intended reader** means acknowledging your reader's perspective or frame of reference. How well you communicate depends on your recognizing that your perspective differs from the perspective of any of your readers, and that their perspectives differ from each other. You will communicate effectively with any reader to the degree that you can reconcile these differences as you write.

Writing to a reader entails using the **reader's implied question** as a guide to presenting and developing your organizing idea. Readers can learn something new only if they are able to relate it to what they already know. Your task, therefore, is to develop the significance of your information in such a way that your reader will be able to recognize a new pattern of relationships.

There are two reasons for focusing on a reader. The first reason is to keep the reader reading. If you do not anticipate your intended reader's perspective, you will not communicate. The second reason is to simplify the task of writing. It is easier and faster to discover what you want to say when you let your reader's perspective guide you in selecting and organizing your information. Your audience naturally benefits from such consideration. But you also benefit from using the reader's implied question in discovering the significance of what you are trying to say.

The **common reader** is an all-purpose audience that you create on the basis of characteristics that most readers share. You can use the common reader when you are writing to an unknown individual or group. The characteristics that the common reader represents are often more reliable than those of a known person.

The most important characteristic of the common reader is ignorance of your organizing idea. The common reader does not know your organizing idea until you have conveyed it. A second important characteristic is impatience. This reader wants to know your organizing idea as soon as you discover it.

The common reader also has three minor characteristics: this reader has achieved about the same level of maturity you have, has reached your level of formal education, and knows as much as you do about your subject—but not about your organizing idea.

The common reader is a convenient construct. It forces you to recognize a frame of reference similar to yours but different from yours. Heeding the demands of the common reader prevents you from writing to yourself, which denies communication, and orients you to another perspective, which enables communication.

Functional evidence is the information that most clearly and persuasively conveys your organizing idea to some intended reader. To find functional evidence, you decide on a set of information that most effectively communicates your organizing idea in terms of your reader's frame of reference. Functional evidence supports or clarifies your organizing idea in a way that enables a reader to comprehend it.

Understanding the concepts of Part 2 is necessary to understanding the concepts of later chapters. If you are not certain about what they mean or what purpose they have, you may wish to consult your instructor before going on. As you proceed, focus your attention on what happens when you write. As you grow more familiar with the writing process, you can learn to recognize and use your own natural writing habits to the best advantage.

The Concepts of Part 2: An Illustration

Consider the following writing situation. You are a junior staff member in your fifth year with CBA, Incorporated, a large consulting agency based in Chicago, specializing in business management and computer software design. Your agency's policy toward staff is to allow a maximum of six years' service before a mandatory decision is made either to promote individuals to partnerships or to release them from the company. Unfortunately, only one staff member in four can be retained in any given year, regardless of the quality of eligible candidates. Though your work has been satisfactory, you have just been notified that you will not receive a partnership. You must seek a new position for the following year.

A partner at CBA with whom you are friendly has told you of an opening at your level in Watson Consulting, a similar agency located in Dallas. This firm needs someone with a degree in computer technology or business management and three to five years of experience in field consulting assignments, preferably as a supervisor. It also wants a person with well-developed communication skills, since a large part of the job involves writing proposals for installing computerized systems in small businesses and also writing reports once the projects are completed. You have many of the skills, and at least some of the experience, that Watson is looking for, so you have decided to contact the vice president in charge of personnel to inquire about the opening.

Your task is to write a letter applying for this position. You must estimate what your reader, the vice president in charge of personnel, needs to know in order to evaluate your credibility and suitability. You must then select functional evidence to support your request for a position. Here are some characteristics of your intended reader (left column) and some indications of how your knowledge of these characteristics can help you choose and organize information (right column).

INFORMATION ABOUT THE VICE PRESIDENT	WHAT THE INFORMATION TELLS YOU AS A WRITER
1. She is a respected consultant with fourteen years of experience and many substantial projects to her credit.	Therefore, she has a clear understanding of excellence in her field and will not be taken in by vague and self-flattering assertions about your credentials.
2. She has been in her current position as vice president for four years and has also worked in other executive and managerial capacities within the firm.	Therefore, she knows what the company's needs are and what credentials a prospective employee must have to fill those needs. She will not be impressed by generalities but will need detailed information about your academic preparation, your specific responsibilities at CBA, your field experiences as a consultant, and your achievements either in

getting business firms to accept your proposals or in designing the systems that those proposals recommend.

3. She will be reading a large number of applications for the position that Watson Consulting has advertised.

Therefore, she will not be patient with applicants whose letters are long, rambling, and overstated; she will want precise details that distinguish you from other applicants.

You have reviewed your credentials and have listed the following pieces of information, later to become functional evidence as you develop your organizing idea:

1. M.B.A. from Wharton in business management and an undergraduate degree in mathematics
2. an on-site supervisor during one consulting project, a computerized billing-system installation at Griggs in Evanston
3. cannot remain at CBA, Incorporated
4. have drafted numerous proposals for installing and updating business systems, more than 60 percent of which have resulted in contracts won by CBA
5. married; wife is originally from Houston
6. written numerous reports on finished projects, even though you were not usually the head of the consulting team
7. happy to come to Dallas for an interview
8. twelve important consulting assignments over the past three years, in addition to the assignment on which you were the supervisor
9. names of several companies for which you worked as a consultant are available, if Watson would like evidence of your expertise

ORGANIZING IDEA

I would like you to consider my credentials for a position with Watson Consulting.

STATEMENT TO THE VICE PRESIDENT

(The numbers in parentheses refer to the pieces of information in the list above. Notice how the information is used in the statement. It is not always literally repeated from the list; instead, it is modified and adapted to suit your purpose as you discover what you want to say within the developing context.)

I am presently employed by CBA, Incorporated, in Chicago, working mainly in computerized billing systems and serving as an on-site consultant to several small businesses in the greater Chicago area (2, 8). However, I will be leaving CBA at the end of this year (3), and I understand from John Franklin, a partner in our firm, that Watson Consulting anticipates an opening at my level around the same time. I am writing to you in the hope that my credentials might be suitable for a position with your company.

I have been with CBA for the past five years, first working in the office drafting proposals for systems installation projects, then, during the last three years, serving on site as a member of several consulting teams and lately as a team supervisor (2, 4, 8). I have written nearly two dozen proposals for introducing or updating computerized billing systems, more than 60 percent of which have resulted in contracts won by CBA (4). I have also written, or assisted in writing, numerous reports on finished projects (6), two of which have been cited as models of reporting format and have been included in CBA's staff handbook. I have served on twelve important consulting assignments in the field, including a major software design project for Carley Inc. of Green Park, Illinois. For the past six months, I have been supervisor of a team installing two new billing systems at Griggs in Evanston (2). If you would find the information helpful, I can supply the names of executives at Carley and Griggs who will testify to my work with their companies (9).

My enclosed résumé mentions that I received my M.B.A. from Wharton in 1976, but my particular interest there was business management. I also have a B.S. in mathematics from Illinois with a concentration in computer technology (1). I am married without children and actually quite eager to find a position somewhere in your area since my wife is from Houston and would like to live closer to home (5).

If my credentials appear acceptable, may I hear from you? I will send my dossier at your request, and I would naturally be delighted to come to Dallas for an interview should you decide that one can be arranged (7).

Applying the Concepts: Part 2

You can apply the concepts presented in Part 2 by analyzing the intended audiences of different magazines. All magazine writers have a clear sense of what readership they are addressing. By reading several articles in the same magazine, you can readily infer the characteristics of its audience. You and your classmates might wish to share issues of the magazines you already have on hand, or you might buy a variety of magazines from your local newsstand.

Once you have a collection of magazines, see if you can answer the following questions. What kind of audience does each magazine address? For example, what are the shared characteristics of the readers who buy *Atlantic* and *Harper's*? How might those readers differ, if at all, from the ones who buy *Esquire*? Are *Sports Illustrated* and *Popular Mechanics* addressed to a similar readership? Can you explain your answers to these questions? What features of these magazines lead you to infer different audiences? Their advertisements? Their distinct styles of writing? Their selection of articles?

What kind of reader might be attracted to any of the following magazines?

Self	*Mademoiselle*
Vogue	*Ms.*
Cosmopolitan	*New Woman*

What similar reader characteristics might any two of these magazines address? Which reader characteristics differ in the same two magazines? Does any one of these magazines address a wider readership than any other? How can you make such a judgment? If you find two articles in different magazines addressing the same subject, what differences are there, if any, between the kinds of evidence selected to support the organizing idea of each article? Answering these questions will depend on your finding clues to the various ways in which the writers use information as evidence; group discussions will probably help you to evaluate these clues.

Your analysis of different magazine audiences might help you in the following writing task. Suppose that you are a free-lance writer—someone who writes for a living—and you are preparing an article about a subject that interests you. Choose any subject you like, or else try one of these: "the hazards of smoking," "the mystical experience," "legalizing marijuana," "games people play," or "the blurring of sex roles." Choose a magazine that might be interested in your topic; you can make such a decision by glancing at the subjects a particular magazine has covered within the last three months. (Your library is a good resource for back issues of magazines.)

Then briefly describe the audience your chosen magazine addresses, listing four or five significant traits of that audience. Once you have identified your reader, you are ready to write your article. Remember to choose only the information that supports your organizing idea while accommodating your reader's implied questions. You will be more likely to use functional evidence if you focus on the following questions as you draft your statement:

1. Does the evidence used in your statement accommodate your readers' needs and expectations, as they were characterized in your description of the magazine's audience?
2. Does the information that you have chosen to support your organizing idea effectively convey that organizing idea?
3. Does your statement acknowledge your intended readers without compromising the development of your organizing idea?

A Comprehensive Writing Task

The following writing situation will help you assess your ability to anticipate the different needs of readers by writing and rewriting. It is a simulated situation; that is, the situation is fictitious but realistic. In this situation, your task is to play the role of an assistant principal of a high school, writing a letter to the parents of a student who was suspended because of a disciplinary problem. The situation presents you with many different clues and also with many different decisions to make about what to say and where and how to say it. Performing this task will show you the subtleties of writing to a reader.

Here is the situation. It is nine o'clock Monday morning. You have been away from your office since last Wednesday on a three-day assignment as part of a team evaluating another city school. In your absence, the principal has taken over your responsibilities in addition to his own. You have finished taking care of late arrivals and can now turn your attention to problems that collected during your absence. The most urgent problem concerns Stephen Davis, a student whom the principal suspended last Friday. You have on your desk several different kinds of information to help you evaluate the problem. These data include a detailed report of the incident leading to the suspension, a note from the secretary that Stephen's parents have telephoned, Stephen's records, and information you have gathered from Stephen's guidance counselor and instructors.

According to the report, Stephen took from the library a reference book plainly marked "for library use only," a book that was needed by all students in a social studies class. When the book disappeared, the social studies teacher questioned several students, including Stephen, who had been in the library immediately before the theft. All denied having taken the book, but the teacher was suspicious. After obtaining permission from the principal, she had Stephen's locker opened. The book was inside. Presented with the evidence of the theft, Stephen used "threatening and obscene language" to the teacher. The incident was witnessed by three students. The teacher then sent Stephen to the principal, who ordered a suspension. The principal instructed Stephen to return in three days with his parents.

Your secretary's note indicates that Stephen's parents have already called this morning. They are quite upset about the suspension and understandably perplexed, since Stephen has never been suspended before. The note also indicates that Stephen told them that he was suspended because of an overdue library book.

Stephen's records indicate that his past academic performance has been erratic, and his grades so far this semester also reveal inconsistencies. He has received an *A* in science, a *C* in social studies, and a *C+* in English. He also has a *D* average in math, although he earned a *B* in math in junior high school.

The guidance office has contributed the following information about Stephen:

◇ He is sixteen years old.
◇ He has two sisters; one graduated last June; she was an honor student, active in class organizations.
◇ His father owns a contracting business in a nearby city. He makes a good living, although he is not a college graduate.
◇ Stephen's mother has long been active in civic affairs and was recently named to the city planning board.

Reports from different instructors about Stephen's behavior provide more information, but it seems to be conflicting. His science teacher, whom you met in the teacher's lounge, says that he is one of the most serious students in the class and that his science project, a hydraulic pump, shows more creativity than he has seen in several years. Stephen's guidance counselor indicates that he has been placed in detention three times in the past semester, twice for excessive talking in English class and once for the same offense in math class. She admits that she has seen him only once in order to discuss his schedule, and that he appeared to be "pleasant" and "rather quiet." Finally, with all this information in mind, you talk to the social studies teacher, who indicates that Stephen had not presented any disciplinary problem in social studies prior to this incident. You perceive, while talking to this instructor, that he is upset because he has not had any such difficulty with students before.

You now have to write the parents to inform them of the situation before scheduling a conference for everyone involved. You want to describe the situation accurately, making clear why their son was suspended, yet you also want to ask their help in dealing with their son's problem. At the same time, you want to avoid simply redirecting their anger away from the school administration and toward their son. In short, you want to find a creative solution to the problem that will address Stephen's needs and his parents' concerns, as well as those of the staff of your school.

With all this in mind, write a letter to Stephen Davis's parents. The task is complex, and it will demand both your ingenuity and your sensitivity to communicate gracefully and to achieve your purposes without alienating your audience.

While planning your writing and constructing your first draft, you might want to consider several questions. What is the role of an assistant principal? Is it merely to discipline students, or is it to help solve their problems? What are the concerns of Stephen's parents? Do they want a detailed justification of the suspension? Are they likely to be interested in working out a good solution? What approach to the problem will be most productive for Stephen? How can you respond at the same time to Stephen's needs, to those of his parents, and to those of the school you represent?

Because this writing situation is complex, you will probably not be fully satisfied with your first draft; you will want to revise, perhaps more than once. Discussing your first draft with your instructor or reading it to fellow students for their reactions will help you to make improvements. In your discussion of this writing task, consider the following questions:

1. What are your various purposes? What are the needs of all parties: Stephen, his parents, and your school?
2. What must you recognize about the situation and point of view of Stephen's parents?
3. How does that recognition assist you in making the choices you do?
4. What are your readers' implied questions?
5. Does the information you have selected qualify as functional evidence?

Part 3: Developing an Extended Statement

8. Forecasting a Written Statement

Part 3, "Developing an Extended Statement," will explain how to organize written statements that are longer than a single paragraph. In the next four chapters, we will show how you can combine a series of paragraphs, thereby developing a line of reasoning. To simplify the explanation, we will break down the extensive process of writing a longer statement into separate, manageable tasks. The first of these tasks is to begin an extended statement by forecasting its significance to an intended reader.

There are many ways of introducing an extended statement, but they all require some sort of forecasting of the assertions you will include in your statement. Your reader will have trouble following your line of reasoning unless you provide some guideline—some sense of direction—to begin with. More important, building a forecast will help *you* even more than it helps the reader; it will help organize the various assertions you will attempt to relate to one another.

Why Write a Forecast?

Unless your readers know where you plan to direct their attention, they may not stay around to consider what you have to say. They are wholly dependent on your forecast for recognizing and following the logic of what you are about to communicate. They also rely on it for perceiving the connection between what they already know about your subject and what you intend to say that is new to them. Of course, your tentative organizing idea will be one of the first indicators of the direction of your line of reasoning, and that tentative organizing idea is therefore precisely what you should include as part of your forecast.

As we saw in Chapter 6, any reader is ignorant of the writer's organizing idea and impatient to learn what it is. Readers will continue to read only as long as they are quite clear about the direction—and the usefulness—of your line of reasoning. They can wait to learn your developed organizing idea until you indicate what it is—but only if you forecast some sense of it at the beginning. You will also need to reinforce this sense of direction in your statement by anticipating the kinds of issues you will address and the order in which you plan to treat them. Readers depend on these features of your forecast to understand the basic structure of the extended statement you intend to present.

Although you are capable of remembering a great deal of information, your ability—and your reader's ability—to integrate a lot of information into a coherent whole is limited. Six or seven items are generally all that a person can remember at one time without losing track. Yet even an essay of only five or six paragraphs may include thirty or forty sentences with at least that many assertions—far more than a reader can manage without assistance. And the longer the essay, the greater the number of assertions. Therefore, it is far easier for the reader and the writer to remember a few major groups or categories of information—which in turn predict many more individual assertions—than to remember an entire sequence of assertions. So, in addition to the tentative organizing idea, writers also forecast a few large categories of information that will later be specifically related in some way. This chapter will show you how to make these categories of information and how to use them to support your organizing idea.

What Is a Forecast?

In order to forecast an extended statement for your benefit and your reader's, the beginning of your statement should contain the following indicators of the territory that you think you will cover. Note that these are only indicators, since you usually do not know at the beginning everything you will discover as you write.

1. YOUR TENTATIVE ORGANIZING IDEA

By now the notion of an organizing idea of a paragraph should be thoroughly familiar to you. It is a comprehensive assertion, stated or implied, to which all of the other assertions in the paragraph relate in some way. The organizing idea unifies the other assertions in a paragraph. But if you are writing many paragraphs, one after the other, how do you unify that longer statement? How are all the separate paragraphs related to each other? The answer to this question is easy. Simply extend your notion of the organizing idea. Just as an organizing idea unifies assertions in a paragraph, it can also unify a series of paragraphs, that is, an extended written statement. When an organizing idea unifies an extended statement, it is necessary to present your organizing idea somewhat differently than if you were organizing merely one paragraph.

In order to unify an extended statement by means of an organizing idea, you will need to present it early in your statement, that is, in your forecast. In most cases, you will need to state it explicitly. These two strategies—presenting an organizing idea in your forecast and stating it explicitly—will make it easier for you to unify each of the separate paragraphs in your extended statement. It will also help your reader to follow your line of reasoning.

Even though you state the organizing idea instead of implying it, it may nevertheless be only a tentative statement. In this sense, the early tentative organizing idea of an extended statement is consistent with what you already know about the organizing idea of a paragraph. As we explained in Chapter 2, the organizing idea of a paragraph evolves from a tentative status to a developed status. This dynamic characteristic of an organizing idea applies to an extended statement as well as to a paragraph; the organizing idea of an extended statement also evolves, and naturally so, since an extended statement is composed of a series of paragraphs.

This provisional nature of an organizing idea is what makes it possible for you to incorporate new insights into your extended statement while still keeping that statement unified for your reader. In most cases, you will not have all of those insights at the start; some of them will occur to you only as you write. So stating a tentative organizing idea in your forecast, a comprehensive assertion that may change as you write, is your way of providing for any later discoveries that you may wish to include in your statement.

To summarize, here is the rationale for presenting a tentative organizing idea in your forecast. Ideally, you would like to tell the reader exactly what you are going to say. But not knowing it, you settle for the next best thing: you make an assertion, one that may evolve, that indicates the most accurate relationship you can find among the pieces of information that are available to you on the subject. Your tentative organizing idea is not static; it becomes progressively clearer to you as you find more relationships among the pieces of information that you are incorporating into your extended statement.

2. CATEGORIES OF INFORMATION

Even when you write a paragraph or two, you may have some difficulty organizing your information, but that task is far more difficult when you are writing an extended statement. When writing a paragraph, you probably can remember which information you have included and which information remains to be included, but when you are writing a longer statement, you may lose track of your information: you may ramble, repeat what you have already said, or even contradict yourself. You will find it far easier to maintain a line of reasoning, to keep track of your information, if you categorize your information at the start. **To categorize your information** is to infer some mutual connections among pieces of information and to state each of those connections in a word or short phrase.

3. THE SEQUENCE OF CATEGORIES

The **sequence of categories** in any extended statement is determined by the order in which the writer names them in the forecast. You determine this order by deciding which sequence most effectively conveys your organizing idea to your intended reader. You may decide, after writing a draft or two, to revise your sequence. At the conclusion of your draft, you may decide, for example, that one category of information will more effectively support your organizing idea if it comes first, not last. Or you may decide that your reader needs to know the information in one category before he or she can cope with information in another category.

These three indicators are basic to the forecast of any statement that you write. The reader needs all of them in order to follow your line of reasoning. The length of your forecast can vary, depending on the extent of your subject and the complexity of what you want to say about it. If your overall statement is likely to be less than eight to ten paragraphs, you can probably include all three of these indicators in your first paragraph. For a longer statement, your forecast might extend to two or three paragraphs. For a book-length statement, it could possibly be the entire first chapter. Experienced writers may even postpone one indicator or another to create expectation and heighten suspense. In any case, a forecast is complete when it presents these three indicators.

There are many ways of presenting these elements, and how you present them is a matter of choice, depending on how you want to guide your readers. In later chapters of this book, you will have a chance to see forecasts that provide different emphases and thereby guide the reader differently. As you will see, some forecasts limit the reader to a narrowing series of assertions that specify in detail what the organizing idea asserts. Others invite the reader to explore implications of the organizing idea, helping the reader to anticipate further assertions that may occur later in the extended statement. In any case, variations of the three indicators in any forecast are a function of the reader's needs. Your reference for building a forecast to suit your purpose—no matter what your purpose—is always your reader's implied question.

Analyzing a Sample Forecast

Suppose you want to write an essay describing Darwin's theory of natural selection to a group of readers who are well educated but are not scientists. You already have a tentative idea about the significance of Darwin's theory, and you want to assert this significance. From your reading, you also have some information that you plan to arrange into categories or blocks of information.

You realize in a general way that your information falls into five categories, the five aspects of Darwin's theory. You do not know precisely how these five aspects affect one another, and you may not know precisely what you will conclude about the information you have arranged. Nevertheless, once you have a tentative organizing idea, some categories of information, and a tentative sequence of these categories, you are ready to write your forecast.

The following paragraph is an example of a forecast with all indicators in place. (The sentences are numbered for easy reference.)

(1) Darwin's theory of natural selection explains better than any other model the various processes of evolution. (2) It explains what the processes are and how they have worked over the centuries. (3) Darwin's theory was highly controversial during the nineteenth century, but it is now accepted in most scientific circles

as the best available explanation of the data that relates to evolution. (4) The theory can be divided into five distinct aspects: overproduction, struggle for existence, variation, survival of the fittest, and origin of new species through inheritance of successful variations. (5) Although these aspects are interrelated and mutually dependent, they can be distinguished for purposes of examination.

Notice the ways in which this paragraph forecasts both a tentative organizing idea and a tentative sequence. The first sentence, predicting how the writer will evaluate Darwin's ideas later, is the tentative organizing idea. The second sentence specifies details implied in the first. The third sentence broadens the context: it suggests that the theory has scientific currency and that it provides a reliable explanation of evolution.

The last two sentences forecast the scope and sequence of what will follow. Sentence 4 names the five aspects (that is, categories of information) to be considered in the analysis of Darwin's theory. It prepares the reader for the specific assertions to follow and indicates the order of their presentation. The fifth sentence gives the reader a glimpse of the way the writer regards the five parts of the sequence—as interconnected natural processes.

You will elaborate on each of these five sentences later in your statement, but you need something to start with. Together these sentences convey (1) your tentative organizing idea, (2) the categories of information that you are going to address, and (3) the tentative order in which you will address them. **To forecast a written statement,** then, is to include these three indicators at the beginning of your statement.

Building a Sample Forecast

Suppose that in a sociology course you have been studying changing customs and mores. Your current reading assignments have directed you to information about contemporary changes in American lifestyles. Your instructor has asked you to write a paper based on your reading that provides an answer to the following question: what effect do contemporary changes in lifestyles have on the individual? You realize that your instructor values fresh and original ideas but also insists on a well-structured essay that effectively integrates available information. Although your instructor has not specified a particular audience for this essay, you know, from comments on other papers you have written for this class, that you are supposed to address an intelligent audience, one similar to the common reader.

After carefully studying your readings, you make a list that contains information you plan to use in your response to the question.

1. declining birthrate
2. consumer protection
3. vacation pay
4. work: valuable or profitable?
5. increasing number of divorces
6. more people living alone
7. the three-career family: his, hers, raising children
8. the working mother
9. early retirement
10. equal pay for equal work
11. nursing home versus hospice care
12. four-day workweek
13. women managers
14. save the whales
15. rent, not own
16. the ugly environment
17. jogging three miles a day
18. civil rights for everyone

Starting with this information, in whatever order you wish, you could derive a tentative organizing idea and also a set of categories that would begin to organize this information. If you are not quite certain of even a tentative organizing idea, you could search the list and derive the categories first. Here, for example, are four labels, naming four categories that subsume all eighteen items on the list. At this early stage, no particular order is necessary.

FAMILIAL INVOLVEMENT

5. increasing number of divorces
11. nursing homes versus hospice care
8. the working mother
7. the three-career family: his, hers, raising children

WORK

9. early retirement
12. four-day workweek
3. vacation pay
4. work: valuable or profitable?
13. women managers

SENSE OF SELF
1. declining birthrate
6. more people living alone
15. rent, not own
17. jogging three miles a day

PARTICIPATION IN SOCIETY
2. consumer protection
10. equal pay for equal work
16. the ugly environment
18. civil rights for everyone
14. save the whales

After studying these categories of information, you might derive this tentative organizing idea:

In making decisions about a personal lifestyle, an individual often encounters stress.

Here is a paragraph that forecasts your response to your instructor's question. As you read it, notice the three indicators it contains: a tentative organizing idea, the four categories of information, and a sense of the sequence in which they will occur.

Recent cultural changes have profoundly affected personal values, causing many Americans to question traditional mores and customs and, in some cases, even to reject them. Because these changes have occurred gradually and unevenly, a traditional approach to lifestyle often coexists with other options that reflect a more revolutionary approach. Although individuals have more freedom in selecting their own lifestyles, they also have to accept the responsibility for any decisions they make. Because these decisions affect some of the most prominent concerns about day-to-day living—sense of self, familial involvement, work, and participation in society—they cannot be made haphazardly; they are interrelated, and they often involve deep feelings as well as opinions. The result is that individuals, engaged in making decisions that will affect their style of life in the future, often encounter stress.

This paragraph is merely one way of organizing the items listed above. There are many possibilities, but the success of any variation depends on how clearly it presents the tentative organizing idea and the information pertaining to it as the written statement proceeds.

Summary

The beginning of an extended statement guides your reader by forecasting in general what is to follow. By making certain indicators explicit, the forecast will also help you to plan the presentation of the information to follow, including even the information that you may not yet have perceived as particularly useful or compelling. These indicators are a tentative organizing idea, the categories of information pertaining to it, and the order in which these categories will probably occur.

Applying the Concept: Forecasting an Extended Statement

Most conventional forecasts reveal the same strategies. Weather reports or predictions of results on election day are examples of forecasting. Previews of movies and advertisements for coming issues of magazines are also examples of forecasting. Studying these examples can help you to understand the function of forecasting in writing. After you have analyzed some of these forecasts, try making a forecast of some statement you wish to write. You might want to work with other students, choosing a topic, gathering information, categorizing it, and describing the categories. Or you might decide to work independently, sharing your own work and insights after you have written your forecast.

The following example may suggest ways in which you and your classmates can apply forecasting strategies; this example demonstrates one way of imposing order on what appears to be a chaos of information. The example will be more meaningful to you if, as you read it, you work with a topic of your choice, following a similar procedure.

Given the topic "the *me generation*," a writer might first jot down some appropriate information in a fragmentary and disordered fashion, concerned at this stage only with generating useful ideas. The following list represents what a particular writer assembled.

1. time and effort required to achieve self-fulfillment
2. knowing how you feel important to decision making
3. competition for schools, jobs, sports
4. people condemn the current generation for its apparent selfishness
5. fast-paced world
6. goals
7. pressure to achieve

8. asserting yourself is necessary
9. lack of concern for others

  After compiling a list, a writer searches for ways to connect the information. Although the writer scrutinizes the information to discover relationships, an organizing idea may not be readily apparent at the start. If it is not apparent, then a useful step is to try to group items of information that seem to belong together. Doing so should enable a writer to make some assertions within each group or category and thereby move closer to the discovery of a tentative organizing idea. Looking at the pieces of information, can you propose some categories into which they may be grouped? There are, of course, many possibilities, depending on how you analyze the information. A particular writer might find that the following three categories—attitudes toward, characteristics of, and reasons for the me generation—would accomplish several purposes. The information might then be grouped as follows:

ATTITUDES TOWARD THE "ME GENERATION"

4. people condemn the current generation for its apparent selfishness
9. lack of concern for others

CHARACTERISTICS OF THE "ME GENERATION"

1. time and effort required to achieve self-fulfillment
2. knowing how you feel important to decision making
6. goals
8. asserting yourself is necessary

REASONS FOR THE BEHAVIOR OF THE "ME GENERATION"

3. competition for schools, jobs, sports
5. fast-paced world
7. pressure to achieve

  At this point, a writer may be ready to pose a tentative organizing idea that connects the categories: "Those who view the 'me generation' as selfish and egotistic fail to recognize that such behavior may be the result of the excessive competition that this generation has had to endure." It is probably now possible for the writer to offer a forecast for a statement about this topic, one that includes both an organizing idea and a preview of its categories of information, that is, of the issues it will treat.

Now draft a forecast of the topic you have chosen. You may want to ask yourself the following questions to guide you in revision. If you and your classmates wish to assess one another's drafts, these questions can serve as a useful focus for discussion.

1. Does your forecast contain a tentative organizing idea?
2. Does it establish the scope of your discussion by means of its introduction of your categories?
3. Does it suggest a tentative sequence for these categories?

9. The Nature of an Extended Statement

Chapter 8 described the building of a forecast at the beginning of an extended written statement. It also described three indicators of a forecast, the most important of which are the tentative organizing idea and the categories of information that the writer plans to develop.

The advantage of forecasting is that it channels your ideas. A forecast limits the countless number of assertions that could pertain to your subject. You may recall the statement at the beginning of this book that writing is a learning process. Simply by writing assertions about a subject, you will discover more to say about it. Not all that you might discover, however, will be relevant to your purpose or purposes in writing. So you will need some way of estimating the range of assertions that will be relevant, and some way of anticipating your estimate can help both you and your reader. Since the process of stating relationships is open-ended, building a forecast will help to establish reasonable limits for what you will write.

The open-ended nature of writing is a force that influences the composing of an extended statement. Any system of assertions could become open-ended, leading the writer to explore ideas in various directions. Some writers, in fact, deliberately use free writing—composing strings of assertions by random association in order to explore a subject. This practice is typical of journal writing or of writing a first draft. But when the writer is ready to communicate, some type of forecast will be needed, especially for an extended statement. The writer will want to make a commitment to some tentative organizing idea and to establish some limits within which it will be possible to explore the consequences of that idea.

What Is an Extended Statement?

An **extended statement** is a line of reasoning, that is, a logical progression from one assertion to another, that begins with a forecast of some sort and concludes when the writer's purpose is fulfilled. Writing any extended statement entails the building of a pattern of assertions that establish the writer's position. Such a construction requires that the writer make reasoned choices among the many assertions that might be related to the subject. When you write an extended statement, you are continuously involved in making such choices. You choose what to include and what to exclude; you choose what to say first and what to say next; you choose to combine those ideas that are closely related and to separate those that are not. Ideally, the assertions you choose will increasingly clarify the significance of what you want to express. Your reasoned choices result in your making assertions that support and develop your purpose or purposes, thereby clarifying the significance of what you want to express.

Using Assertions to Construct an Extended Statement

A statement of any length is made up of assertions, its smallest units. The nature of assertions was discussed in Chapter 1, which defined an assertion as the statement of some relationship derived from separate pieces of information. As you recall from that chapter, an assertion typically occurs in the form of a sentence because the conventions of writing make it necessary to compose in sentences.

A second fact about assertions is important to remember in order to understand the nature of an extended statement. Some assertions fulfill a special role: they link other assertions together. Chapter 2 described the organizing idea of a paragraph as its major assertion. The assertion is *major* in the sense that it provides a relationship central to all the other relationships expressed in the paragraph. The organizing idea provides some way of showing how the other assertions are related to it and to one another. Because it links all the assertions in a paragraph, the organizing idea is the paragraph's most comprehensive statement of relationship.

When that comprehensive relationship is actually *stated*, as Chapter 2 pointed out, the organizing idea is explicit; as the writer, you can state the organizing idea anywhere in the paragraph. But you can also build a paragraph—a related set of assertions—in such a way as to *imply* its organizing idea. In such a case, the assertions lead the reader to infer the organizing idea; that is, the reader decides what the comprehensive relationship is from the way the other relationships overlap.

So far we have been reviewing the role of the organizing idea of a paragraph. In any unified paragraph, one major assertion focuses on the relationships established by the other assertions. But the concept of an organizing idea is not limited to a paragraph; it can extend to unified statements of any length, even if they incorporate many paragraphs. It can even extend to a unified statement that has many chapters, such as a book.

Any extended, continuous statement presents an organizing idea. In fact, the tentative organizing idea of an extended statement is developed by the organizing ideas of each successive paragraph. But before discussing the development of an organizing idea, we will show how a paragraph—a relatively short statement—can imply an organizing idea.

The paragraph below contains six assertions that together imply an organizing idea. For your reference, the assertions are numbered as sentences. Assertions 2, 3, 4, and 5 expand on assertion 1; they specify the consequences of the condition stated by the first assertion, and they extend these consequences in successive order. Assertion 6 draws a conclusion from the relationships that are stated in assertions 2 through 5.

> (1) A substantial minority of today's population is gay. (2) Many homosexuals, who are members of this significant minority, go through much of their lives feeling miserable, sensing their alienation from the straight majority. (3) Because these individuals know that some members of society condemn their sexual preferences, they often choose to lead two separate lives: a straight life as their social facade, a gay life only among their friends. (4) The alternative is to risk public ridicule, defamation of character, and even bodily injury. (5) The gay community, in other words, suffers the same indignities and the same disenfranchisement that other suppressed minority groups are forced to endure in this country. (6) And these indignities will continue until gays unite and claim the rights and privileges they deserve.

This paragraph implies an organizing idea that is broader than any one of its assertions. Even the writer's conclusion (that indignities will continue to occur until gays unite) grows out of the larger notion that

homosexuals are a persecuted minority. Together these assertions imply a more comprehensive assertion, which might be stated in this way:
"Homosexuals in our society will suffer discrimination, disenfranchise-
ment, and alienation, as do other oppressed minority groups, until
they unite and demand their rights and privileges." This implied organizing idea could probably be stated in different ways, but in any
case it is broader than any one of the assertions that contribute to it.
Moreover, its meaning has accumulated from the successive assertions
that are linked to each other.

   An implied organizing idea tends to evolve through the accumula-
tion of other assertions, as this example indicates. This organizing idea
grows out of a series of assertions. To review: assertion 1 specifies the
status of the gay population, which assertions 2, 3, and 4 progressively
extend and refine. Assertion 5 summarizes all the preceding details of
this status, and assertion 6 refines assertion 5. The link between these
two is the word *indignities,* which then becomes the subject of an even
more extended, more specified assertion about the status of the gay
community.

The Organizing Idea of an Extended Statement

Any written statement that reflects the writer's reasoned choices is a
system of assertions. The statement may be merely a paragraph, or it
may be more extended, composed of seven or eight—or more—paragraphs. The above statement about the gay minority, which happens
to be a paragraph, conveys an organizing idea because it is a system of
assertions. Organizing ideas are not confined to paragraphs; extended
statements also convey organizing ideas.

   An organizing idea, stated or implied, is whatever assertion makes a
string of assertions coherent. It is a comprehensive assertion that sub-
sumes other assertions in the statement; that is, it converts them into a
subordinate, supporting status. An organizing idea is therefore the
unifying assertion in any string of assertions, whether those assertions
become a paragraph or a series of paragraphs. If the above statement
about the gay minority were extended to seven or eight paragraphs,
for example, then the sequence of its seven or eight organizing ideas
would convey yet another, more comprehensive organizing idea that
would focus on the whole statement.

   An extended statement is not merely a compilation of static units,
however; it is dynamic. An extended statement is composed of para-

graphs that establish a flow or a continuity of reasoning. The concept of a flow of ideas or assertions suggests that each idea evolves, in turn, from the sum of all the ideas preceding it. Viewed in this manner, an extended statement is like the course of a river that is fed by smaller streams along the way. Each of these tributaries adds to the volume of the river, which broadens or narrows or deepens as it changes direction along its course. And this analogy to a river suggests the importance of the tentative organizing idea that begins the extended statement. Like the headwaters of a river, the tentative organizing idea is modest, unstable in force at first, and it develops only as the contributing ideas merge with it along the way.

With your knowledge of assertions, you can now understand more precisely what an extended statement is and what it does. An extended statement is a system of assertions in which each assertion depends on others before and after it. In such a statement, one finds a continuity of ideas or assertions, which head toward some resolution or conclusion.

Later chapters in Part 3, on the diminishing and expanding sequences, will describe how assertions can either narrow or broaden an extended statement. Meanwhile, the rest of this chapter concerns the ways in which the forecast of an extended statement can help the writer generate the major assertions that will follow in that statement.

Using Your Forecast to Generate an Extended Statement

Writers interrelate assertions whenever they compose a string of sentences that might become a paragraph or an extended statement. But this process becomes more complex when the writer is developing an extended statement. The complexity results from the writer's need to control an increasing number of assertions, even while generating them. To meet this need, skilled writers typically employ some deliberate procedure that channels assertions into a line of reasoning.

Forecasting is one useful way of channeling assertions. A forecast will help you to control assertions even as you write them. When you construct a forecast, your tentative organizing idea and your brief mention of the categories that you propose to discuss allow you to make a broad survey of those aspects of your subject that you intend to write about. These elements in your forecast will help you to address your reader's implied questions.

Once you have a forecast, you are ready to begin developing your extended statement. The assertions you will generate about each category in your forecast may comprise one paragraph or more; you probably will not know ahead of time how many there will be—or even what they will be. But as soon as possible, try to derive an organizing idea for each of your proposed categories of information. As Chapters 1 and 2 explained, you derive such a major assertion from your assembled list of information fragments, first by searching for some relationship among specific items on the list and then by asserting that relationship. This major assertion is useful for organizing the other, subordinate assertions you will make from the remaining, relevant information on the list for that category.

Since you will be discovering as you write, do not be surprised if your first drafts are not entirely satisfactory. For example, you might generate an organizing idea for a paragraph that does not support or clarify the tentative organizing idea in your forecast. In that case, you might decide to discard some of the assertions in that paragraph. Or you might create a string of sentences that contains enough assertions for more than one paragraph. In that case, you will probably want to regroup the assertions you have drafted.

Keeping your forecast in mind will help you to revise your extended statement as you are writing it or in a later draft. By surveying your initial sense of the significance of the tentative organizing idea contained in your forecast, you can channel your assertions into a system of relationships that best fulfills your purpose. You channel them by asking yourself how what you are now drafting relates to your original purpose.

You might even decide as you write that your forecast needs amendment. In that case, feel free to amend it. You might realize that one of the categories of information you originally intended to develop is not very useful; it may not yield the kinds of assertions that would best support your position. If so, remove the category. Or you may decide to refine your tentative organizing idea; it may be more or less comprehensive than it should be. If so, refine it. The more you use these strategies of revision, the more precise your interrelationships of assertions will be.

The following example illustrates how you can use a forecast to create an extended statement that is a system of assertions. Suppose you plan to write a statement about guns because you perceive the violent use of guns as an urgent problem that demands action. Realizing that you first need to gather information about your subject, you list the following:

◇ right to bear arms—constitutional right
◇ accidents during heated family arguments
◇ not even hunters or collectors handle guns safely
◇ hunting accidents
◇ guns for protection
◇ availability of guns
◇ stolen guns
◇ children are innocent victims
◇ misuse of guns is a social problem
◇ inadequate preparation of hunters

At this stage of your planning, your purpose may not be entirely clear to you. (As Chapter 3 pointed out, several different purposes may have motivated your writing, all of them relevant to the situation, yet leading in too many conflicting directions. Planning your extended statement consists partly of reconciling your several purposes.) Since your feelings are strong, you might easily move toward a tentative organizing idea—perhaps this one: "It is time to consider what action should be taken by elected officials to deal with the widespread misuse of guns." This idea encompasses several of your purposes for writing an extended statement. You have already learned that you can use your intended reader to help you refine and clarify your primary purpose. (Chapter 5, you will recall, talked about readers' frames of reference; Chapter 6 explained that readers formulate an implied question about your subject and your organizing idea based on their own frames of reference.)

To plan efficiently, you will need to think of your reader at this point so that you can guess at this reader's implied question. The implied question will not only help you clarify your primary purpose in writing but it will also guide you in choosing additional evidence, that is, some further information to support your tentative organizing idea. (Chapter 4 described the way in which your organizing idea and your evidence support each other as you write, and Chapter 7 described strategies for focusing this evidence on your reader's implied question.) Using these concepts to help you plan your extended statement, you decide on the intended reader to whom you will address this statement.

Suppose your reader is the junior senator from your state, recently the victim of an armed robbery in his own home. Election time is drawing near. He must take a position on gun-control legislation, one of the major issues that concern his constituents. The senator's implied question might be, "What do the voters of this state think about gun control?" Formulating this question can help you define your primary purpose.

Now that you have a reader and a tentative organizing idea in mind, your next task is to analyze the information you listed and to arrange it into possible categories. You can, of course, list the categories in whatever order you wish.

◇ concern about availability of guns
◇ criminal use of guns
◇ mishandling of guns by hunters and collectors
◇ accidents with guns in the home

Having decided on a tentative organizing idea and a set of categories of information, you can now write the first draft of your forecast. It might look like this:

> Many people are understandably concerned about the widespread availability of guns in American society. This availability, they argue, must be restricted in order to reduce violence and to ensure public safety. Considerable evidence from trials throughout the country indicates that many acts of violence are directly related to guns. Thousands of people every day abuse the right to handle a gun—not only criminals, but also hunters, collectors, and other usually law-abiding people. It is now time to consider what action should be taken by our elected officials to deal with the widespread misuse of guns.

Using this first draft of your forecast, you can begin to make assertions within each category of information that you plan to include. As you write paragraphs and evolve explicit or implicit organizing ideas for them, you may find it useful to look back at your forecast in order to channel your assertions into an appropriate line of reasoning.

If you decide to focus first on the category of "mishandling of guns by hunters and collectors," you might select these pieces of information to expand into assertions:

◇ hunting accidents
◇ inadequate preparation of hunters
◇ not even hunters or collectors handle guns safely

Your first draft of the paragraph might look like this:

Even hunters and collectors are not safe from acts of violence related to guns. Each year during the hunting season, inexperienced hunters unintentionally maim or kill other hunters or innocent people whom they mistake for game. Many hunters and collectors, not adequately instructed in the proper handling of guns, wound themselves—sometimes fatally—because they do not know how to clean their weapons. Some way must be found to convince hunters and collectors that the mishandling of guns can result in regrettable violence.

Thus you can see the procedure for developing the tentative organizing idea of your forecast in the mainstream of your extended statement. As you write, you continue to generate assertions and organizing ideas of paragraphs, category by category, until you arrive at a significant conclusion, at which point you stop writing. The tasks of thoughtfully constructing assertions about each category and ordering them in sequences will help you generate a coherent statement.

To continue your statement, you might want to write another paragraph on the same category of information, "mishandling of guns by hunters and collectors," or on one of the other categories of information listed on p. 118. You will find that some of the assertions can serve as organizing ideas for paragraphs; others will turn out to be subordinate assertions. Some assertions may generate new ideas that could provide materials for several paragraphs. For example, you might want to mention presidential assassinations and the dangers of mentally disturbed people resorting to guns. You might even want to discard some of your assertions because they would take too much time to relate to the tentative organizing idea stated in your forecast. All these options are open to you as you write, and choosing among them makes it possible to be much more precise in writing than you could ever be in speaking.

Summary

After you have gathered a list of information, developed categories, and written a forecast for your reader, you are ready to make further assertions about your subject. With your forecast as a guide, you continue to write paragraphs in which you generate new assertions about various categories of information. These assertions make clear specific relationships that you feel are key to your extended statement. As a line of reasoning, an extended statement logically progresses from one assertion to another, indicating a direction and moving toward some eventual destination.

Applying the Concept: An Extended Statement

You have already applied the concept of forecasting to your writing. At this point you are ready to organize an extended statement, starting with a forecast and then extending the forecast into a system of assertions. Begin by selecting some topic that interests you and your classmates. A timely issue will probably serve your purpose best, since such issues are generally controversial and often generate different responses from different writers. Perhaps you are a soap opera addict and want to argue that these stories provide a harmless means of escape from responsibility. Or perhaps you do not smoke and want to make a statement about the dangers to people who do. Or perhaps you care about the energy crisis and want to argue that most Americans need to change their wasteful habits. Many other topics are also suitable: teen-age alcoholism, mind-expanding drugs, women in business, the draft, capital punishment, euthanasia, or the American way of dying. But only you can decide which subject you feel strongly about and want to develop. Discussing various topics in class may help you and your fellow students decide which topic you each want to write about.

Once you have a subject, list your information, organize it in appropriate categories, and then state a tentative organizing idea. Now you are ready to look at your categories of information and to decide which one you want to talk about first. For example, if your subject is abortion, you may have initially considered as a tentative organizing idea that "an informed person can make a more intelligent decision about abortion than an uninformed person." While scanning your information, you may have categorized it according to the physical, psychological, social, and ethical aspects of abortions, and you may have decided to discuss the physical aspects first.

After you have chosen your subject and have written your forecast, write one or more paragraphs that organize the information in your first category. It is important to remember that you should not merely describe that category but that you should relate whatever you say to the tentative organizing idea of your extended statement. For example, if you were writing about abortion, you might ask yourself how the physical effects of abortion support or apply to what you are arguing. Your answer to this question may yield an organizing idea for a paragraph about physical effects. By asking and answering such questions repeatedly as you write, you can more closely connect subordinate assertions to your tentative organizing idea. You will therefore have created a more tightly organized system of assertions.

Since this chapter concerns the relationship between the forecast and the system of assertions it channels into a line of reasoning, you and your classmates might read one another's drafts and suggest how the writer might clarify this relationship or support an initial position by additional assertions. You might want to test whether or not the connections you believe you have established are clear to your readers. Sharing your own writing and making suggestions about how to revise will help all of you do more careful rewriting. You can then clarify confusing assertions and insert missing links into your line of reasoning.

Keeping the following questions in mind as you revise will help you to focus on the relationship between your tentative organizing idea and all your other assertions. If you and your classmates decide to assess these drafts as a group, these questions will provide a useful focus for discussion.

1. Did the writer use the forecast as a guide in developing the subsequent paragraphs supporting the tentative organizing idea?
2. Are the links between the tentative organizing idea and the organizing ideas of individual paragraphs evident to a reader?
3. Are the links between subordinate assertions also explicit?
4. Is the direction of the extended statement clearly stated in the forecast and maintained in subsequent paragraphs?

10. The Diminishing Sequence

In Chapter 8, we discussed the forecast statement, describing the three indicators you can use to anticipate your probable line of reasoning. These indicators are a tentative organizing idea, a brief indication of the categories of information that you will later present, and the sequence of these categories. In Chapter 9, we discussed the extension of this forecast into a system of assertions that support your line of reasoning; that chapter described the usefulness of generating an organizing idea for each of the separate categories of information that you propose to cover.

While you are developing your forecast, you will be faced with a major decision about the sequence of your extended statement, that is, about the order in which you will present the categories you have chosen to discuss. This order, or sequence, will contribute to the effectiveness of your extended statement and its appeal to the reader. The sequence you choose will depend partly on your purpose, partly on your reader, and partly on the amount of information available to you. Although you will have opportunities along the way to modify your sequence, you will need to know your options when you start. This chapter and the one following it describe these options—the diminishing and expanding sequences. We will introduce each and explain how to establish a sequence that will help you achieve your purpose.

Language, Sequence, and Reader

Unlike the information in a snapshot or a painting, the pieces of information in a verbal statement are not revealed all at once. They are revealed as a linear succession of events that are separate but related. Pieces of information—expressed in words, phrases, sentences, paragraphs, and groups of paragraphs—overlap each other in complex ways. Sentence by sentence, paragraph by paragraph, your statement evolves in time, developing from one assertion to the next until you are satisfied that your statement is as complete as possible.

Because verbal structures are linear, your task as a writer is to construct the most effective sequence for the information you want to present. You choose an order for your various pieces of information; you decide what should come first and what should follow, and you make this decision repeatedly as you write. Fortunately, you can look to your intended reader for help in deciding on a sequence of information. Just as you can use the reader's frame of reference to choose evidence (as described in Chapter 7), you can also use the reader's frame of reference to guide you in ordering that evidence throughout every paragraph of your evolving statement.

Usually, readers proceed by associating the new evidence presented in an extended statement with whatever information is already known to them. But readers cannot cope with new information presented in just any sequence. In order to make the associations between new and old, they need to know your most significant assertions before they can make use of less important ones. A sequence of assertions will make sense to the reader only to the degree that it accommodates this need.

What Is a Diminishing Sequence?

The reader's implied question about your organizing idea ("What will this mean to me?"), provides you with the simplest and most efficient guideline for building a sequence. You can present your information in an order that satisfies the requirements of your intended reader. There are two obvious advantages in constructing a sequence with your reader's needs in mind: it saves time for the reader, and it shortens your writing time. If you know the significance of what you have to say, you can get started more quickly, write more rapidly, and convey your organizing idea with less effort. In order to find a sequence that fulfills the reader's needs, you will need a clear sense of your categories of information.

As soon as you label your categories, you can forecast them in a diminishing order of importance, according to what you perceive to be the needs of your intended reader. Presenting your categories in a di-

minishing order of importance in your forecast predicts the way you
will present assertions in your extended statement. When you present
information in a diminishing order, you are developing a **diminishing
sequence;** that is, you are developing a sequence in which you will
present important information first and less important information
later.

The model that news writers follow, sometimes called the inverted
pyramid, is the most familiar example of the diminishing sequence.
News writers use this model because it gives them a ready means of
presenting information; they begin with what the reader most needs to
know, and then they provide relevant information in a decreasing order of importance.

The inverted pyramid primarily provides for the reader's needs.
Only secondarily does it provide for the writer's process of discovery.
In fact, it can even constrain the writer's discovery process. The news
story favors the priorities of the reader over the priorities of the writer.

To use this diminishing sequence, therefore, is to invert the result of
your natural learning process. You first present a tentative organizing
idea about your information to accommodate the priorities of the
reader. You begin your statement with an indication of the significance
of what you are about to relate and the direction in which you will explore your subject. Your reader first needs to know your organizing
idea before comprehending the importance of any single piece of information. By revealing the significance of your information as soon as
possible, therefore, you make your statement easier to follow. Your
reader's estimate of the value of any piece of evidence will be far more
accurate if you have first stated the organizing idea that the evidence
is designed to support.

The inverted pyramid can be diagrammed. First assume that the
writer's learning process is represented by the figure of a normal pyramid. This figure signifies that the writer usually moves toward a developed conclusion that is broader than the tentative organizing idea:

WRITER'S PRIORITIES

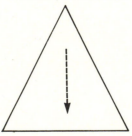

The reader's priorities can then be represented by an inverted pyramid:

READER'S PRIORITIES

This figure reflects the reader's need to know about the conclusion before comprehending the relevance of the separate pieces of information.

Inverting your natural writing process will anticipate the needs of your intended reader. In other words, you invert Model I of the learning process to achieve Model II:

MODEL I   MODEL II

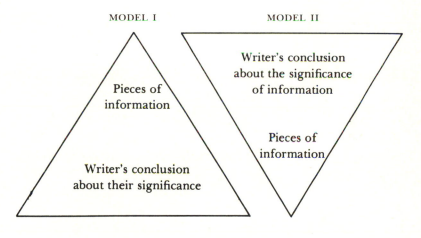

In news writing, the reader's desire to know the writer's most significant assertion dictates the sequence of information. The news story proceeds from the most significant assertion to the least significant assertion. As you read through a typical news story, you find that more and more is said about less and less; the importance of the information diminishes as you proceed. The typical news story can be diagrammed this way:

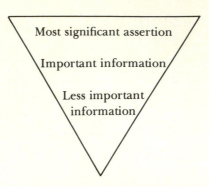

As an example, consider the following set of information. Which of the items would be the most significant piece of information to a newspaper reader? Which would be the least?

1. It has been snowing for a week in Denver.
2. Plane carries load of Christmas mail.
3. Plane develops trouble with navigational equipment.
4. Plane approaches landing in Denver.
5. Plane is observed to be off course.
6. Plane crashes.

These events are listed as they occurred in chronological sequence. But the order in which the events occurred would not satisfy the newspaper reader's sense of their significance. A news story would probably begin with the fact that the plane crashed (6), since this is what the reader would need to know in order to understand the relevance of the other pieces of information in the set.

Items 3, about navigational equipment, 4, about the landing approach, and 5, about the error in the plane's course, are important details, though not necessarily in that order. (Of course, if it were a Denver newspaper, 4 would suddenly become much more important information, given the perspective of a Denver newspaper reader.) Items 1, about the weather, and 2, about Christmas mail, are less significant.

The news writer's sequence, an inverted pyramid, would probably be something like this:

6. Plane crashes.
3. Plane develops trouble with navigational equipment.
4. Plane approaches landing in Denver.
5. Plane is observed to be off course.

1. It has been snowing for a week in Denver.
2. Plane carries load of Christmas mail.

Although the sequence is not absolutely fixed—writers might differ about the placement of one item or another—the general direction is from the crash itself, as the most significant assertion, to the least significant, the plane's cargo. Notice again that the newspaper sequence is not based on chronology but on the reader's sense of what is significant. This acknowledgement of the reader's perspective is the essence of the inverted pyramid.

It is important to know when the inversion of the reader's and writer's priorities is appropriate. Although one naturally learns more about one's subject as one writes, the diminishing sequence constrains the writer's capacity to grow in understanding. For this reason, the diminishing sequence is an appropriate sequence to use for particular kinds of writing—those in which inversion is not a difficult task for the writer. It is ideal for writing that primarily conveys facts or specific details, such as a newspaper story, a business letter or memo, or an essay exam in any subject. These modes are useful to the writer who has a good grasp of the information to be presented and who knows reasonably well what needs to be stated about that information.

If you are writing a short piece, one composed of only a few paragraphs, you will probably not include all three of the indicators in a forecast. You will need to include your organizing idea, since developing a diminishing sequence requires that your most significant assertions come first. But you probably will not include your categories (nor, therefore, any indication of their sequence), since your reader can readily determine them merely by reading a few paragraphs.

But if you are writing a diminishing sequence that is an extended statement, you will need to guide your reader to an understanding of all relevant information. And as Chapter 8 indicates, there is no better way to guide your reader than by writing a complete forecast—one that contains the scope of your line of reasoning and all three indicators of its direction.

The Diminishing Sequence in Detail

The assertions that follow could provide a basis for an actual news story; they have been listed in random order to illustrate how a diminishing sequence is constructed. Suppose that your task is to discover a

sequence for these assertions based on the inverted pyramid and to explain the rationale for that sequence. Here are the steps in this task.
See if you can perform them before looking at the solution.

1. Find an assertion that can serve as an organizing idea for this news
   story.
2. Find an assertion that lists categories of information in a diminishing sequence.
3. Group the remaining assertions into categories of related information by listing the item numbers in appropriate columns.
4. Briefly describe why you arranged the categories of information as
   you did.

SET OF ASSERTIONS

1. Armstrong found that the lunar surface was "very, very fine
   grain," a "sandy surface."
2. Planting the flag did not make the moon America's territory; under the treaty signed by eighty nations, the moon belongs to all human beings.
3. With millions throughout the world watching the black-and-white
   television pictures they beamed back, Armstrong and Aldrin
   landed on the moon, planted the American flag, and explored the
   moon's surface.
4. America's two moon pioneers completed the first exploration of
   the lunar surface today and sealed themselves back in their spaceship Eagle for the hazardous voyage home.
5. They used specially designed scoops to gather rocks, dirt, and core
   samples from the surface.
6. The flight captured the imagination not only of Americans but
   also of people around the world.
7. On Earth, 142 scientists from many different countries were wait-
   ing to study the samples to see if they would give any clue to the
   origin of the moon and the universe.
8. Pravda said, "The courageous cosmonauts have landed on the
   moon," but it gave bigger headlines to its still mysterious Luna 15,
   which remained in the lunar orbit.
9. Armstrong backed down a ladder on the lunar module and
   planted his left foot on the surface.
10. First, the samples will have to spend twenty-one days in quarantine.

11. "That's one small step for man—one giant leap for mankind," Armstrong said.
12. The astronauts explored the gray, alien surface of rocks, hills, ridges, and dust that turned their boots cocoa-colored.
13. Armstrong and Aldrin planted the American flag.

Now fill in the following outline:
An assertion that can serve as an organizing idea:

_____

_____

_____

An assertion that indicates the sequence of categories of information:

_____

_____

_____

Assertions listed in diminishing order of importance:

Block I	Block II	Block III	Block IV	Block V
_____	_____	_____	_____	_____
_____	_____	_____	_____	_____
_____	_____	_____	_____	_____
_____	_____	_____	_____	_____

Here is one possible sequence of information that you might choose:

ORGANIZING IDEA: 4. America's two moon pioneers completed the first exploration of the lunar surface today and sealed themselves back in their spaceship Eagle for the hazardous voyage home.

SEQUENCE OF CATEGORIES OF INFORMATION: 3. With millions throughout the world watching the black-and-white television pictures they beamed back, Armstrong and Aldrin landed on the moon, planted the American flag, and explored the moon's surface.

Assertions listed in diminishing order of importance:

Block I	Block II	Block III	Block IV	Block V
6	9	13	12	5
8	11	2	1	7
				10

If you suggested a smiliar sequence, your rationale might have been as follows: Block I reveals the international implications of the event. Block II describes Armstrong's landing on the moon and his memorable statement about the first step he took on its surface. Block III describes the planting of the flag and the meaning of that event. Block IV describes the initial exploration of the moon's surface. Block V describes the gathering of the rocks and their scientific importance.

The sequence outlined above is not the only possible way in which these information pieces could be arranged. For example, if you were organizing this information for a group of international lawyers, you would probably place the assertions describing the flag-raising ceremony earlier. If you were writing to a group of scientists, you would probably include the information about the rocks earlier in your statement.

Summary

Making effective sequences of information depends on your realizing that writing and reading are linear activities. The writer must decide what to say first and what to postpone until later. Meanwhile, the reader is wholly dependent on what comes first for understanding everything that follows.

Recognizing that your reader's priorities are different from your own can help guide you in establishing a sequence. You can use your reader's perspective to help you order your information. One way to use your reader's perspective is to establish a diminishing sequence, in which the reader's needs are primary and the writer's process of discovery is secondary.

Applying the Concept: The Diminishing Sequence

You and your classmates can perceive the advantages of the diminishing sequence by gathering news stories and analyzing the order in which writers have presented their information. Try to gather news stories from different newspapers and also from different sections of the same newspaper (though not from the editorial page, since its articles are less likely to follow a diminishing sequence). Guess the intended reader or type of reader for each news story, and derive an implied question for that reader or type of reader.

Recalling the features of the diminishing sequence, you might check first to see if the organizing idea appears early in the news story you are examining. Does this most significant assertion answer the reader's implied question? Next, try to name or label the categories of information that the writer is using to support the organizing idea. After you have a clear sense of the categories of information, you might pose some questions about the order in which they appear. Which category, for example, contains the most significant information? Where is that category placed in the article? Which category contains the least significant information? Where is that category placed in the article?

Remember that the sequence of categories and the organizing idea reflect the writer's sense of the reader's priorities. As you read a news story, can you imagine other possible sequences? Would these other sequences alter the reader's response to the story? What assumptions about the reader's priorities might these other proposed sequences suggest to you? Suppose you wrote down the individual assertions in a news story in random order. Could you and your classmates approximate its original sequence? Try it.

Once you have studied samples of the diminishing sequence, you may want to construct one about another subject. With your instructor's permission, you and your classmates might work together, discussing the various decisions about the order of the sequence you will make. Your task entails arranging categories of information according to the model of the diminishing sequence. To speed up the process of your writing, define your readers and their possible interests at the start. Your reader's implied question will help you decide quickly which assertions are most significant and which are least.

Try to choose a subject that depends heavily on the arrangement of facts or details, such as those presented in a newspaper article. You may decide to play the role of a newspaper reporter who has observed some significant happening, or you may decide to relate some newsworthy incident that you were actually involved in. As soon as you have decided on a subject, list as many details as you can imagine or recall, whichever is appropriate. Then list some assertions based on your information that will become the building blocks of your article. Choose one of these to be your organizing idea. As soon as you have exhausted the number of assertions you can make about your data, select some categories that further organize your assertions and arrange these categories—and the assertions within them—in a diminishing sequence.

You are now ready to draft your article. You may want to use the following questions to help you assess what you write. These questions also may be used to provide a focus for group discussion.

1. Does the organizing idea, the most significant assertion, appear early in the statement?
2. Are the categories of information evident to the reader?
3. Does the sequence evolve from the most significant assertion to the least significant assertion?

11. The Controlled Expanding Sequence

In Chapter 10 we described a diminishing sequence of assertions, a sequence primarily oriented to the reader. The writer presents each assertion in an order that reflects as closely as possible the reader's sense of priorities and interests. Starting with the most important statement of relationship, the writer moves in order from more important to less important assertions until all the information has been presented.

Any extended statement, to be coherent, must follow some sequence, and the diminishing sequence is one possibility. But since you write for different purposes at different times, you will want to choose a sequence that matches your purpose. The expanding sequence offers you another possibility.

In this chapter, we will explain how you can build an expanding sequence, one that lets you explore your subject, that enables you to discover new relationships as you write. Discovery is natural to the writing process, but in order to communicate what you discover, you will need to control your expanding sequence of assertions. Therefore, we will also explain how you can build a controlled expanding sequence, since gaining control of the writing process is crucially important to the writer.

Establishing an Appropriate Sequence

The usefulness of a diminishing sequence or an expanding sequence depends on the purpose you want your extended statement to achieve. The diminishing sequence strongly channels the flow of assertions, whereas the expanding sequence favors the growth and development of an organizing idea. The former stresses the delivery of factual or detailed information; the latter stresses the writer's discovery of new implications that increase the significance of what has already been stated. The expanding sequence, however, presents the writer with a more flexible order and therefore with a more complex task of control, which the writer needs to establish at the start.

Your control of an expanding sequence lies primarily in the way you write your forecast. That forecast will, of course, include three indicators: a tentative organizing idea, categories of information, and their tentative order. But the way you present these indicators, specifically, the way you address the reader's implied question, is what determines your control over the assertions that will expand your statement. You address this question one way when you write a diminishing sequence and another way when you write an expanding sequence.

The difference between forecasting one sequence and forecasting the other is subtle but distinct. When you forecast a diminishing sequence, you imply that successive assertions will be restricted to the relationship stated in the tentative organizing idea. In forecasting an expanding sequence, on the other hand, you imply that successive assertions will state new relationships that are implied in the tentative organizing idea.

This distinction determines the differing characteristics of the two sequences. Since the assertions in a diminishing sequence are limited to a supporting or clarifying role, the tentative organizing idea is not likely to change very much throughout this type of sequence. But in the expanding sequence, successive assertions explore and extend the tentative organizing idea, thereby causing it to change and develop.

The Two Sequences: An Illustration

An efficient way to explain the expanding sequence is to compare it to a diminishing sequence, illustrating how each proceeds differently from the same tentative organizing idea. For this illustration, here is an assertion that will do as a tentative organizing idea: "Massive frauds have been discovered in the city's nursing homes." First we will see how a news writer might use this statement in presenting a diminishing sequence.

1. Massive frauds have been discovered in the city's nursing homes.
2. The central figure in the inquiry is John Smith, the director of health services.
3. Smith has not yet been available for questioning.
4. Investigations were made to discover the fraud in nursing homes.
5. Elvira Jones, deputy attorney general, led the probes.
6. Investigating the homes was a grim experience, Jones said later; she could not believe her eyes.
7. Patients were mistreated.

Assertion 1 is the most comprehensive assertion in the set. The meaning of each of the other assertions depends on it in some way and is therefore limited by it. Moreover, each of the other assertions tends to depend on its predecessor on the list. The nature of the sequence, therefore, is a diminishing order of importance. The news writer has followed a specified set order, moving from most to least important information on the list, thereby accommodating the reader's priorities.

A different way of proceeding is to discover what you mean as you write, which is a method natural to the writer, rather than to follow a set formula. Each assertion that you write about any subject not only conveys the relationships that you are already aware of but also suggests further relationships that could be stated about the subject. So you naturally try another assertion to relate new and old information, and that new assertion is necessarily dependent on the one before it. By this process, the meaning of your assertions accumulates, and you begin to see a significance in your subject that you had not originally seen.

An **expanding sequence** is any written statement that represents a growth in the development of your understanding; in such a sequence, later assertions are likely to be more important than earlier ones because they reflect a clearer awareness of what you are trying to say. By permitting new discoveries, the expanding sequence allows for a conclusion that is more significant than any assertion that has led up to it, a conclusion that represents a new awareness of the significance of your tentative organizing idea. The advantage of the expanding sequence is that it enables you to learn as you go.

Here is a schematic illustration of what happens in the expanding sequence; it begins with the same assertion, about the discovery of frauds in the nursing homes, that was used in the previous example of a diminishing sequence. In contrast to the diminishing sequence, how-

ever, the expanding sequence becomes more comprehensive with each
new assertion.

1. Massive frauds have been discovered in the city's nursing homes.
2. The extent of these frauds is widespread and shocking.
3. Older persons live in filthy conditions, receive little care, and simply
   wait to die.
4. Society has left its senior citizens to die out of sight and out of mind.
5. Children no longer assume the burdens of caring for their parents,
   leaving them prey to unscrupulous nursing home operators.
6. Neglect of older citizens may be interpreted as another sign of the
   deterioration of responsibility in an indifferent society.

Note how each new assertion goes beyond its predecessor on the list,
rather than being subordinate to it. Unlike the assertions in the diminishing sequence, each assertion in this sequence adds new information
that makes explicit what the previous assertions only implied. Conse-
quently, assertion 6 is more comprehensive and more significant than
anything expressed in earlier assertions. The writer's conclusion is not
merely that the elderly receive poor care; rather, it is that poor care of
the elderly suggests the deterioration of social responsibility in our cul-
ture. The writer has discovered something new about the subject simply by following the implications of each previous assertion.

This example of an expanding sequence illustrates the way in which
writing can be a learning process. No single assertion is definitive,
fixed, or entirely resolved, no matter how reasonable or conclusive it
may seem to a reader. To the writer, every assertion contains within it
some suggestion of how it might be extended or expanded or refined.

In a writer's statement, every assertion represents some unfinished
business. Try making an assertion about any subject, and see how easy
it is to start a train of thought. Simply by declaring a relationship, you
will perceive how it suggests other relationships. The words you use to
state this relationship will signal other information, assertions, and ref-
erences that you have already stored. In this way, each assertion reveals to the writer the possibility of saying more, of moving toward a
richer, more resonant conclusion than was, at first, apparent.

To summarize, each sequence presents you with a different advantage. The diminishing sequence helps you to accommodate the
reader's needs efficiently. It is useful in writing essay exams, for example, because it forces you to begin with what you think your instructor wants to know (in this case, the reader's *stated* question). It is useful

in all formal correspondence, particularly in business letters and memos, because it maintains a focus and tends toward brevity. It is useful in writing any short statement for which you know most of the information at the start.

The expanding sequence, on the other hand, enables you to begin a statement without knowing exactly what you want to convey, to explore your meaning as you write, and to end by saying all that you mean. The expanded sequence is useful in any extended statement or in any statement that involves more than simple, obvious relationships. This sequence enables you to use the writing process as a learning process.

The Controlled Expanding Sequence

The most promising way to control an expanding sequence is to combine the advantages of both sequences in the same written statement. If you can do this, you will have a **controlled expanding sequence;** you will be able to explore your subject as fully as you wish and to arrive at the full meaning of what you want to say, doing so efficiently and satisfying the reader's needs at the same time. With this strategy, you make use of your natural tendency to explore and discover first by forecasting the possibilities of expansion and then by keeping your reader informed of your learning process as it occurs. Combining both sequences allows you to satisfy yourself as well as to satisfy your reader.

To see how all this can be done, recall the two figures of pyramids in Chapter 10, representing the different learning processes of the reader and the writer.

READER'S LEARNING PROCESS: WRITER'S LEARNING PROCESS:

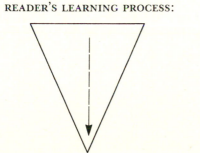
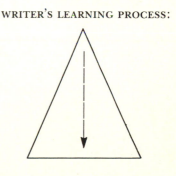

The reader's pyramid signifies a learning process that moves from an organizing idea to subordinate assertions in a diminishing sequence.

The writer's pyramid also signifies a learning process, but one that entails the discovery of new significance by means of making and relating assertions. In terms of these two triangles, the strategy for accommodating both you and your reader is to superimpose the reader's inverted pyramid on the writer's pyramid. The resulting figure looks something like an hourglass.

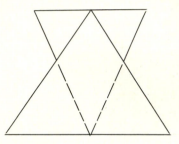

Stated in terms of priorities, the strategy is to begin with the reader's priorities in order to get started. Specifically, you begin with a forecast that helps your reader anticipate the significance of your organizing idea. As we have already indicated, the way in which you answer your reader's implied question makes it possible to predict that you will explore the implications of your organizing idea. But you need not be exclusively concerned with the expectations of your reader. In fact, you can be equally concerned with your own process of discovery, with your own movement from tentative organizing idea to developed conclusion. And think of the bonus that this strategy offers you: look again at the hourglass figure, and notice that the bottom baseline is longer than the top.

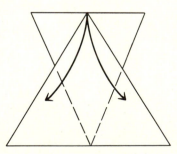

The base of the writer's pyramid, where you ultimately arrive, is broader than the base of the reader's inverted pyramid, where you started. The broader base of the writer's pyramid represents the bonus of a conclusion to your first draft that you did not anticipate when you began to write that draft.

By continuing your reader's implied question as you write, you make new assertions that expand your earlier understanding and may go surprisingly beyond it. You reach this new understanding by continuing to heed your reader's implied question. You reveal to the reader the new discoveries you make as you discuss each new category of information until you finally recognize your conclusion.

The combined reader-writer sequence allows you to write with more control and with a better sense of direction; it enables you to make appropriate choices as you write. Finally, the combined sequence yields a conclusion that has evolved beyond your tentative organizing idea without requiring you to revise your forecast.

The Controlled Expanding Sequence: An Illustration

Suppose you decide to write a personal essay about an important change you are contemplating, a prospective change in your whole lifestyle. You are thinking of moving your residence from a suburb to the city. Your prospective move has been seriously questioned by a friend who is a real estate broker and whose livelihood depends on the sale of suburban property. This reader's implied question can be stated in several ways: "What is wrong with the suburbs?" or "Why should anyone move from here?" You want to answer these questions, and you also want to re-examine your own reasons for making the change—reasons that you may not be quite sure of. Suppose that from your own notes and impressions, you have jotted down the following pieces of information and that you now want to write an explanation of your decision.

◇ more varied forms of entertainment in the city
◇ suburban prices geared to relatively high levels of income
◇ better air in the suburbs, more open space
◇ cannot walk to stores and movies in the suburbs
◇ more leisure time in the city, less time commuting
◇ deterioration of the cities
◇ increasing cost of home ownership in the suburbs
◇ privacy in the city

From these information fragments, you form the following tentative organizing idea: "I am returning to the city in order to stay abreast of the changing realities of our environment." As you plan a sequence of what you want to say, you can see that your information falls into these three categories:

◊ disadvantages of city
◊ disadvantages of suburbs
◊ possibilities of city

Using this sequence of categories and this tentative organizing idea, here is one possible forecast. (Notice that the categories of information in this case happen to precede the tentative organizing idea.)

> Not too long ago, many Americans moved to the suburbs for good reason. We were responding to the realities of our environment; the cities were becoming uninhabitable, and we wanted to escape them. But moving to the suburbs forced us to change our way of living and to make expensive compromises. Now our lifestyles need a different kind of support. We see new possibilities for living well in the city, and it is time to move back. As you see, we are trying to keep abreast of the changing realities of our environment—we are trying to keep up with ourselves.

This forecast states a tentative organizing idea, having already predicted a sequence by which to discuss the categories of information that will develop it. In doing this much, your forecast also does more: it implies a close relationship between one's lifestyle and one's environment. Even as you start to write, your awareness of your subject will start to grow.

Here is one way these assertions about lifestyle and environment might help you to develop another paragraph, specifically, a paragraph about the disadvantages of the city:

> We city dwellers enjoyed the city before it began to deteriorate. I particularly liked to walk along the city blocks, passing through one small neighborhood after another, being either private or public as I wished. We all had space to move around in if we wanted it, and we had relative security too. But even as we enjoyed these values, dirt, noise, and crime on those city blocks began to alienate us. In time, the city environment contradicted our values and the lifestyle we sought.

Notice that this paragraph suggests another assertion, namely, some kind of relationship between lifestyle and values. This same relationship occurs again in the discussion of the next category of information, the disadvantages of the suburbs.

For ten or fifteen years, the new suburban environment supported the lifestyle we valued, but our contentment was only temporary. We spread out in larger homes, but the cost of maintaining these homes has soared beyond our means. We had space to move around in, but this moving around required a certain level of income. If our income falls below this level, we cannot afford this costly environment.

Notice some new assertions in this category of information (the disadvantages of the suburbs) that extend the scope of the paragraph beyond what was originally anticipated, specifically, relationships between costs and benefits. In turn, you might expect that these later assertions will suggest and influence what you write next. The final category in the forecast, the possibilities of the city, might develop in this way:

Our values have remained unchanged over the years. We still want privacy and space to move around in. We still want to thrive in our environment and not be limited by it. For these reasons, many suburbanites are considering a return to the city. We can sell our cars and walk. We can sell our suburban real estate and avoid the cost of home improvements. We do not need to suffer so many new costs and assessments, because the cities already have sewers and shopping centers. We can purchase privacy with our rent, and we can indulge in much of the leisure and cultural enrichment that a city offers, no matter what our income. Given the rich possibilities of the urban environment, it is time to return, time to keep faith with our values. Only in this way can we know who we really are.

In this controlled expanding sequence, each cluster of assertions has provided clues for extending and developing the tentative organizing idea. Every assertion provides some new information that might be extended or modified in a later assertion. This short personal essay makes use of both sequences: it expands and develops its organizing idea, having first alerted the reader to such a possibility.

Summary

In a diminishing sequence, the organizing idea is more comprehensive than the assertions that follow it. In an expanding sequence, the organizing idea is extended and developed beyond its original statement. Your acknowledgement of the reader's implied question can show the reader which sequence is about to occur. Each sequence offers the writer different advantages. It is possible to gain the advantages of both by forecasting the possible expansion of the organizing idea and by using the reader's priorities to organize your categories of information.

Applying the Concept: The Controlled Expanding Sequence

In this chapter we have discussed the relationship between the purpose of an extended statement and the type of sequence—diminishing or expanding—that will best serve your purpose. We have also pointed out that you can establish the type of sequence for the extended statement in the forecast. Within the forecast, you can suggest which sequence you plan to use by acknowledging the reader's implied question. You can either reinforce the relationship stated in the organizing idea, or you can cite some implied relationships in the organizing idea that your extended statement may address.

There are many ways of suggesting either of these sequences, so it is helpful to look for models that establish the nature of the flow of ideas that will follow. Such models are at hand in unexpected places. One model is provided by any well-designed computer program, which is typically a diminishing sequence. The main procedure, which appears first, controls all the subprocedures that follow it, and the documentation of the program makes this sequence explicit. Literary models provide other examples of careful forecasting. Short stories, for example, typically predict the nature of the action to follow. That action usually concerns a conflict of some sort, and some tentative organizing idea will express the conflict. Moreover, the beginning of a short story will often contain clues about how that conflict will be analyzed in the rest of the story.

Lengthy magazine articles are more conventional models for your analysis of ways of predicting a sequence. These articles are typically formed by an expanding sequence. Your instructor or reference librarian can guide your search for examples. Some magazines tend to present essays with strong forecasts, and since the essays run for at least five or six pages, you will have a chance to see how these forecasts control the expanding sequences. Try some articles in *Atlantic Monthly, Fortune, Psychology Today,* or *Scientific American.* Some of the forecasts will be quite explicit, indicating both an organizing idea and formal categories of information. Other essays, which are also expanding sequences, will appear to present only a minimal forecast, gradually revealing a purpose and developing an organizing idea as they proceed. Where would you look for clues about sequence in essays such as these? In any case, after you and your classmates have collected articles from different magazines, you can build a discussion around this series of questions: Which articles were easier to follow, especially in one reading? Was the ease with which you could follow the argument related to the kind of forecast in each article? And how did the forecast establish the sequence that followed?

After you have studied a variety of forecasts for clues about sequence, you might care to analyze one kind of clue we have been discussing in this chapter, that is, the assertion that addresses the reader's implied question. Here is another example of that kind of clue. Suppose that you are writing about the subject of divorce and that your tentative organizing idea is this:

The divorce rate is increasing in the United States.

This assertion sounds definitive when it appears by itself, but as an organizing idea, it is tentative because it has not yet been developed in any way. Given your purpose in making the assertion, whatever that purpose might be, you can acknowledge your reader's implied question—"What will this mean to me?"—as soon as you identify a reader.

If your reader is interested in some sociological significance of the increasing divorce rate, you might categorize your information in terms of population groups (by age, income, or geographical region) so that you can reinforce your assertion with details. A diminishing statement would be appropriate in this case because statistics about divorces in these categories can support or clarify your tentative organizing idea. Acknowledging the reader's implied question, therefore, might take this form:

The divorce rate is increasing in the United States. *This increase reflects changes in the number of divorces in several different population groups.*

By the way it acknowledges your reader's implied question, that second sentence would give you the opportunity to set up your categories in a diminishing sequence.

If your reader is a person about to be married, however, that reader's implied question might reflect an interest in the reasons for divorce and in how to avoid one. Since there are many reasons for almost any divorce, answering this reader's implied question would indicate a need for an expanded statement. Since you cannot write merely a list of reasons for your reader, you will need to categorize them (as they pertain, for example, to personal lifestyle, to raising a family, to money, or to frequent travel and professional commitments). But this reader's question implies a need for some explanation of whatever reasons you might discuss. Your forecast, therefore, would naturally indicate that you propose to explore some causes of divorce. It could begin like this:

> The rate of divorce is increasing in the United States for many reasons. These reasons include personal lifestyle, raising a family, money, or frequent travel and professional commitments. *But merely naming these reasons does not explain how an individual might avoid divorce.*

Notice how the third assertion extends beyond the tentative organizing idea by indicating that there are implications to be dealt with. This extension is the writer's response to this reader's implied question.

Now you can turn your study of all these models to advantage in your own writing. They can even help you practice before you start to write a new paper. Reread one of your old papers written some time ago; analyze the way it begins and the way it develops. And to focus your analysis, you can use these questions:

1. Does the statement present a forecast?
2. Does the forecast address the reader's implied question?
3. In what ways does the forecast convey the sequence of what will follow?
4. Does the extended statement pick up any of the clues in the forecast and extend or expand them?

Review of Part 3

We will now review the concepts you have worked with in Part 3: the concept of forecasting, the nature of an extended statement, and two possible sequences for constructing an extended statement. The diminishing sequence presents the evidence that supports the tentative organizing idea in successive, narrowing stages. The expanding sequence, however, develops the implications of the tentative organizing idea with broader, more extended information. It is possible, however, to gain the advantages of both sequences. The controlled expanding sequence offers the efficient communication of the diminishing sequence and the exploratory freedom of the expanding sequence.

The Essential Concepts of Part 3

An **extended statement** is a system of assertions, supporting a tentative organizing idea, wherein each assertion depends on other assertions before it and anticipates those that follow it. In other words, an extended statement is a line of reasoning. It is a directed movement from one idea to another, leading toward some destination. It is a system of strategic choices designed to convey a unified significance that accomplishes the writer's purposes.

A **forecast** is a preview of the writer's extended statement. Ideally, it presents three indicators of the forthcoming line of reasoning—first, a tentative organizing idea; second, the categories of information the writer expects to address; and third, a sense of the sequence in which those categories will be addressed. Forecasting is a means of orienting the reader; it conveys as much of the writer's meaning as the writer is able to perceive at the start of an extended statement. In addition to acknowledging the reader's need for orientation, it helps the writer to develop a precise line of reasoning.

A **diminishing sequence** describes one possible order for the consecutive assertions in an extended statement. It is an order of descending priorities, wherein the broadest and most important assertions come first. Later assertions in the statement merely elaborate on the more general ones that precede them. In a diminishing sequence, the writer's search for new meaning is subordinate to a concern for efficient communication to the reader. Alternatively, the **expanding sequence** describes a progressive order of assertions, wherein later ones are broader and richer than earlier ones, and represent the writer's growing understanding of the tentative organizing idea introduced at the start.

The **controlled expanding sequence** offers the advantages of both types of sequences: the efficient communication of the diminishing sequence and the exploratory freedom of the expanding sequence. Specifically, the writer begins with a forecast that orients the reader to a tentative organizing idea, thereby preserving the best feature of the diminishing sequence. Thereafter, the writer proceeds to explore the full significance of that idea by evolving an expanding sequence along the lines anticipated in the forecast. As a written statement develops, the writer continues to answer the intended reader's implied questions about the direction of the line of reasoning and about its significance. The writer provides periodic reassurances until both writer and reader can perceive a developed conclusion, representing their new, shared learning. In Part 4, we will explain how these reassurances are provided at various points in your written statement.

The Concepts of Part 3: An Illustration

Following is a completion of the extended statement introduced in Chapter 9 regarding gun control. The statement is a line of reasoning that includes both a forecast and a system of assertions. The system contains features of both the diminishing and the expanding sequence.

You may recall that the subject of the statement is "the violent use of guns" and that its tentative organizing idea is "It is time to consider what action should be taken by our elected officials to deal with the widespread misuse of guns." As you may remember, your reader is the junior senator from your state, who has recently been the victim of armed robbery in his own home. Election time is drawing near; he must take a position about gun-control legislation, one of the major issues among his constituents. You estimate that his implied question might be, "What do the voters in my state think about gun control?"

Your forecast of the statement begins this way:

> Many people are understandably concerned about the widespread availability of guns in American society. This availability, they argue, must be restricted in order to reduce violence and to ensure public safety. Considerable evidence from trials throughout the country indicates that many acts of violence are related to guns. Thousands of people every day abuse the right to handle a gun—not only criminals, but also hunters, collectors, and other usually law-abiding people. It is now time to consider what action should be taken by our elected officials to deal with the widespread misuse of guns.

This forecast includes your tentative organizing idea—that action should be taken by our elected officials to deal with the widespread misuse of guns. It also anticipates your reader's priorities by stating some categories of information and a sequence for their discussion. One category is the criminal abuse of guns. A second is their abuse by hunters and collectors which leads to numerous accidents. A third is their accidental misuse in the home, where the most tragic gun-related fatalities often occur.

You might continue your statement this way:

> Criminals have very little difficulty obtaining the guns they need. They find it relatively easy to purchase them. At times, the guns they use are stolen from the homes of collectors or hunters. Because guns are so readily available, many acts of violence are committed against innocent victims who deserve to be protected.

You have now presented the first aspect of your sequence—the criminal use of guns. You have developed your organizing idea by suggesting that innocent victims need protection. You have also sustained the relationship you established earlier between guns and violence.

Suppose you develop your argument in this manner:

> Even hunters and collectors are not safe from acts of violence related to guns. Each year during the hunting season, inexperienced hunters unintentionally maim or kill other hunters or innocent people whom they mistake for game. Many hunters and

collectors, not adequately instructed in the handling of guns, wound themselves, sometimes fatally—because they do not know how to clean their weapons. Some way must be found to convince hunters and collectors that the mishandling of guns can result in regrettable violence.

Thus, you have developed the second category of your sequence, the mishandling of guns by hunters and collectors. Maintaining the connection between guns and violence, you have also expanded the significance of your organizing idea by suggesting that there must be some way to convince gun users—before they cause violence—that a gun may be a dangerous weapon.

Now suppose you develop the third category of your sequence—misuse of guns by other persons—in this manner:

More disturbing than the violence that criminals, hunters, and collectors inflict on innocent people by their irresponsible handling of guns are the gun-related incidents that occur in the home. Children are often seriously or fatally harmed by guns that their parents use for hunting or protection. There is also a very real danger that a heated family argument may lead to an unpremeditated crime. In fact, violence is a condition that is always possible, and guns simply make is easier to occur.

In continuing the line of reasoning in this way, you have further expanded your equating of guns with violence. By discussing children, the family, and the home, you have provided more evidence for your organizing idea, namely, that it is now time to consider what action should be taken.

Now you need to develop an appropriate conclusion from the system of assertions already in place. Notice how the developed organizing idea expands your line of reasoning by moving beyond an appeal for gun control to a broader concern for the causes of violence in our society.

The misuse of guns by criminals, by hunters and collectors, and by family members reveals that we must direct our energies toward an analysis of the many ways in which violence manifests itself in our society. Guns are only one visible manifestation of this violence. The legislation of gun use will no more protect us from violence than the legislation of speed limits has protected us from violence on the highway. We need to analyze the causes of violence in whatever form it takes. Only then can we institute programs that will deal with the fundamental causes of violence, not merely with its manifestations, and that will help us protect ourselves from violence—intentional or unintentional.

This conclusion completes your line of reasoning, evolving a final and developed assertion from the preceding system of assertions already stated. In Chapter 14, we will explain how to build conclusions that develop beyond what they summarize.

Applying the Concepts: Part 3

One helpful procedure before constructing either a diminishing or expanding sequence is free writing. This is a kind of writing that emphasizes learning rather than communicating. In fact, the results of free writing are often comprehensible only to the writer, not to the reader. The writing portrays the circuitous route of the writer's discovery process. The advantage of free writing is its ability to generate a great variety of ideas, thereby offering you a clearer sense of what is worth writing about in connection with your subject. You can often begin a new writing project with a free-writing exercise that energizes your thinking. But before you can communicate with a reader, you need to shape the results of your free writing into a forecast and a line of reasoning that effectively convey your learning to an intended reader. The following writing task will help you test your ability to explore your subject freely and also to communicate effectively to a reader.

Suppose you and your classmates choose a topic in common, something you have strong feelings about so that you can easily generate discussion, such as "students should or should not be required to take courses outside their field of interest." Or you might want to discuss a question or an issue brought up in your course readings or in a newspaper article. In any case, take a little time in class to air your personal views and hear the opinions of others.

When you have fully discussed the topic, try some free writing. Start with any question you wish to answer about the subject and write down whatever comes to mind about it. You need not worry about the organization of this writing; just let one association lead to another without pausing to work out precise connections. Include everything that occurs to you, even if it appears to be somewhat off the track or irrelevant, and do not stop writing for any elaborate planning or thinking. Try to write in this fashion for fifteen minutes or for as long as there is time.

Without looking back, write a sentence that represents the most important idea you feel you have discovered while exploring your subject. Keep it for future use. Then assess the information that you generated while free writing. Can you select some categories from the information in your free-writing exercise that will group your various insights? Write them down and save them for later. Now look at the assertions in your writing. Can you identify some that are potentially useful? Are others of little or no help? Cross out the unhelpful ones and bracket the useful ones for further reference.

You are now ready to redraft your free-writing exercise with a view toward communicating more efficiently to your reader. You can establish either a diminishing or a controlled expanding sequence. First, write a forecast that states your tentative organizing idea—probably some version of the sentence you wrote after the free-writing exercise, asserting your most important idea. Include also in your forecast the categories of information you selected, and determine the order in which you will present them.

Continue to develop a system of assertions, using materials from the free writing. If you are writing a diminishing sequence, you will want to present your most significant assertions early in your statement, following them with assertions that are successively less significant. Your primary consideration will be your reader's implied question. But if you are writing a controlled expanding sequence, you will want to present your least significant assertions early in your statement, following them with successively more important assertions. Your primary consideration will be your natural process of discovery; you will be able to learn as you write. Having forecast for your reader, however, you will still be able to take his or her needs into account.

As you write your first draft, using either a diminishing sequence or a controlled expanding sequence, the following questions can guide your assessment of its effectiveness:

1. What did you originally want to communicate? What were your original purposes? Which of these purposes now seems most important?
2. Does your tentative organizing idea accommodate your purpose?
3. Who is your intended reader?

4. By what labels have you categorized the information generated by your free writing?
5. In what order have you arranged these categories of information?
6. Which sequence, diminishing or controlled expanding, have you selected to convey your line of reasoning?
7. If the sequence is a diminishing sequence, have you arranged your assertions by beginning with the most significant assertions and concluding with the least significant ones?
8. If your sequence is a controlled expanding sequence, have you arranged your assertions by beginning with the least significant assertions and concluding with the most significant ones?

Part 4: Making an Extended Statement Coherent

12. Monitoring Your Extended Statement

Part 3 concerned the nature of an extended statement and the means of developing it. In Part 4, we will discuss several strategies for ensuring the coherence of a line of reasoning even as you are writing it. The first strategy, described in this chapter, is to monitor your extended statement, that is, to test the way in which it is developing. Another strategy is to overlap assertions so as to maintain the continuity of your line of reasoning by techniques described in Chapter 13. Still another strategy is to conclude your extended statement in a way that is appropriate to the sequence you are developing. Strategies for concluding will be discussed in Chapter 14.

These various strategies provide guidelines for revising your extended statement, for making it more coherent as you progress from one draft to another. Their function is to help you maintain the logic of your line of reasoning as it develops. They are all important means of communicating effectively, of ensuring coherence. But the principal means of ensuring coherence is the monitoring of successive categories of information so that they are carefully interrelated and unified.

When Is an Extended Statement Coherent?

Coherence is a quality of relationship among the parts of any structure or system. *To cohere* literally means "to cling together." If we extend this literal definition, we can say that a system or structure is coherent to the degree that its parts are related to one another in a logical or orderly fashion. Since an extended statement is a system of interrelated assertions about a subject, it is coherent to the degree that it reveals the interrelationships among its assertions. In other words, we may say that an extended statement is coherent to the degree that its sequence is self-evident to the reader.

For the reader, the test of the writer's control is the degree to which the extended statement reveals a pattern among its interrelated assertions. Your reader needs to recognize some pattern among the assertions in order to comprehend the line of reasoning; and by providing a set of signals to remind the reader of the pattern, you reinforce or alter it. Building a set of signals into your line of reasoning as you proceed, therefore, will help you control the logic of your statement and keep your reader informed of that logic.

Monitoring Your Extended Statement

The writer controls an extended statement by monitoring it in roughly the way a navigator plots the moving position of a ship on a voyage. Like the writer, the navigator has a purpose—to get from point A to point N. The journey begins with a tentative formulation of the course the ship will follow to arrive at that destination. The course is charted at the start of the voyage, and it includes a series of tentative arrivals at reference points along the way. Since tide, winds, and currents can be expected to drive the ship off course, the navigator must constantly check the ship's actual position with respect to the reference points initially established. This analogy aptly describes the writer's situation. Upon completing every leg of the journey, the writer can check the direction of the statement.

To monitor an extended statement is to be aware of changes from one category of information to another and to signal these changes to the reader. Simply being aware of the direction you are taking will help you to be more precise in your decisions as you continue. But to keep your reader informed of your reasoning—especially in an extended statement—you should ask periodically a specific question, namely, "How does this category of information relate to my organizing idea?"

There is a simple rationale for this question. You often do not know exactly what you want to say until you have said it, especially in a controlled expanding sequence. But you have already made an estimate of your line of reasoning in your forecast; your tentative organizing idea indicates the approximate destination of your line of reasoning, and you can use it in checking each reference point along the way—to see how the present direction of the extended statement relates to its proposed direction.

The reference points are the intersections of any two categories of information. To check your course at each intersection, you ask yourself how the assertions within a given category of information support your tentative organizing idea. By stating for the reader the answer to that question, you can clearly signal the current direction of your written statement. At any intersection of categories, you can raise this question about the category you have just completed as well as the category you are about to begin.

Monitoring an Extended Statement: An Illustration

The following illustration presents a series of typical decisions that a writer makes when planning, writing, and monitoring an extended statement. These decisions are presented here in abbreviated form, showing enough of the proposed statements to illustrate the procedure of monitoring, that is, of testing and signaling changes in direction.

Assume that the writer's subject is "the problem of differences in the quality of education in urban and suburban schools." The writer addresses a local taxpayer whose implied questions are "How serious is this problem?" and "How readily can it be resolved?" After listing pertinent information, the writer derives this organizing idea:

> The causes of inequities between urban and suburban schools must be considered before we can contemplate a solution.

The writer has also decided that the information on the list falls into these four categories:

◇ description of the problem
◇ lack of funds
◇ sociopolitical biases
◇ effect of biases

With this tentative organizing idea, this sequence of categories, and this intended reader in mind, the writer drafts the following forecast:

> Many concerned individuals, distressed about differences in the quality of education between urban and suburban schools, look

for speedy solutions to these inequities. Unfortunately, the causes are complex and deeply rooted. They are both economic and sociopolitical, and they contribute to alienation. These causes must be considered before we can contemplate a solution.

Before reading the following paragraphs, notice how carefully the writer has forecast the sequence of the categories of information that will develop the tentative organizing idea. In the forecast paragraph, the writer appeals to the reader by answering another version of the the reader's implied question, "How will your organizing idea affect my understanding of your subject?" The writer indicates what the problem is and that the causes of it must be considered before contemplating a solution. Having briefly described the problem, the writer then lists the categories of information in the following sequence: lack of funds, social and political biases, and effect of biases.

In the paragraphs that follow, the writer continues to develop the tentative organizing idea, elaborating on each category in the order that it was forecast. As you read the extended statement, try to see how the writer uses the strategy of monitoring to test the way in which the line of reasoning is developing. Has the writer kept you informed about the direction of the line of reasoning?

Nearly everyone admits that children in the poorer urban schools do not fare as well as their suburban counterparts. Adequate facilities and qualified teachers are provided to children from wealthy homes, whereas inadequate facilities and unqualified teachers are usually provided to children from poorer homes.

The evident shortcomings in urban schools have often been attributed simply to lack of funds. State legislators have argued, for example, that funds are limited in every school system, urban and suburban alike, but that since the urban schools have many more problems, these problems cannot be resolved by the funds that are currently available.

Many economists support this claim, arguing that, if more money were allocated to the urban systems, the quality of the facilities and the instruction would be certain to improve. Unfortunately, they add, the money is simply not available; hence, disadvantaged children remain disadvantaged.

We must realize, however, that the educational dilemma we face is far more than an economic problem. It is rooted in the

American system of values, and any long-range solution will have to be compatible with the subtle attitudes that influence our approach to educational issues.

Received opinion about the sociopolitical history of the public schools indicates that they have been essentially a middle-class instrument used to "Americanize" the people they presume to educate. The public schools have traditionally assumed that their function is to establish for the young what is right, what is customary, what is expected, and what is wrong, in order to impose conformity on American society.

Probably the major underlying cause of shortcomings in urban schools is the fact that school boards throughout the country are dominated by business and professional people who live in the suburbs and who represent the middle class. These school boards do not merely allocate funds; they also rule on what ideas will be taught, what texts will be used, how instructors will teach, and related matters—all reinforcing a middle-class system of values.

Many young people today are resisting this imposition of middle-class values on their own emerging individual and social identities. Black urban schoolchildren in particular may have no interest in moving closer to a social class from which they are somewhat removed.

The essence of the crisis is that minority groups are alienated from political institutions when such institutions no longer reflect the values and hopes of the group. This alienation is exactly what has happened in the urban schools. The poorer, inner-city children who attend these schools resist the instruction they receive from well-meaning but perhaps naive middle-class teachers, and the quality of their educational experience inevitably deteriorates.

A review of this extended statement will help you understand how the strategy of monitoring can be used. The writer forecasts four categories of information, the first of which logically follows from the opening paragraph. The first category, the description of the problem, is discussed in the second paragraph of the statement:

Nearly everyone admits that children in the poorer urban schools do not fare as well as their suburban counterparts. Adequate facilities and qualified teachers are provided to children from wealthy homes, whereas inadequate facilities and unqualified teachers are usually provided to children from poorer homes.

The second category—the lack of funds—logically followed the description of the problem. The writer perceives that the reader needs only a brief reminder of what this new category refers to. Nevertheless, the writer offers a signal about the change of category by mentioning the lack of funds—which had been anticipated in the forecast through a reference to economic causes of inequity.

> The evident shortcomings in urban schools have often been attributed simply to lack of funds. State legislators have argued, for example, that funds are limited in every school system, urban and suburban alike, but that since the urban schools have many more problems, these problems cannot be resolved by the funds that are currently available.
>
> Many economists support this claim, arguing that, if more money were allocated to the urban systems, the quality of the facilities and the instruction would be certain to improve. Unfortunately, they add, the money is simply not available; hence, disadvantaged children remain disadvantaged.

These two paragraphs represent two different views of the problem—the view of legislators and the view of "many economists." Although the views are compatible, the reader might miss the fact that the two views represent one category of information, the lack of funds. So the writer perceives the need to signal the end of this category on funding and the beginning of the next. The first sentence of the next paragraph conveys this signal: "We must realize, however, that the educational dilemma we face is far more than an economic problem."

The next category of information—social and political biases—confirms three different subcategories—the goal of teaching children to conform in the public schools, the political power of middle-class school boards, and black children's resistance to middle-class influences. Since the extended statement is about to change direction, the writer now signals that these three new factors are related to one another and that they represent a single category of information. To identify them as a unit, the writer names their common quality: they concern values that underlie educational issues. The connection is not made in merely one assertion; the writer needs a whole paragraph to convey it. Notice how the line of reasoning turns at the beginning of the first of the four paragraphs that follow. Once the signal is given, the three categories—all aspects of values—can then be explained in two more separate but related paragraphs. Here is the signal of a change in category:

> We must realize, however, that the educational dilemma we face is far more than an economic problem. It is rooted in the American system of values, and any long-range solution will have to be compatible with the subtle attitudes that influence our approach to educational issues.

And here is the three-paragraph development of the new category:

> Received opinion about the sociopolitical history of the public schools indicates that they have been essentially a middle-class instrument used to "Americanize" the people they presume to educate. The public schools have traditionally assumed that their function is to establish for the young what is right, what is customary, what is expected, and what is wrong, in order to impose conformity on American society.
>
> Probably the major underlying cause of shortcomings in urban schools is the fact that school boards throughout the country are dominated by business and professional people who live in the suburbs and who represent the middle class. These school boards do not merely allocate funds; they also rule on what ideas will be taught, what texts will be used, how instructors will teach, and related matters—all reinforcing a middle-class system of values.
>
> Many young people today are resisting this imposition of middle-class values on their own emerging individual and social identities. Black urban schoolchildren in particular may have no interest in moving closer to a social class from which they are somewhat removed.

Continuing to monitor the extended statement closely for the reader, the writer must introduce one final category of information, the effect of biases. Since it immediately follows the causes of the problem—lack of funds and sociopolitical biases—it is easy for the writer to anticipate for the reader the effect of these biases, so only a brief signal is needed.

This signal occurs in the first sentence of the next paragraph, which asserts the "essence of the crisis." This essence is that political institutions are at odds with the values of the very groups for which they are responsible. Then, within the same sentence, the writer asserts a new claim, namely, that in this situation minority groups will be alienated from these political institutions. Within the same sentence, in other words, the writer signals a change in direction by summarizing and then making a new assertion based on the summary. The signal of a summary is printed here in boldface, and the new assertion is printed in italics.

> **The essence of the crisis** is that *minority groups are alienated from political institutions when such institutions no longer reflect the values and hopes of the group.* This alienation is exactly what has happened in the urban schools. The poorer, inner-city children who attend these schools resist the instruction they receive from well-meaning but perhaps naive middle-class teachers, and the quality of their educational experience inevitably deteriorates.

In sum, during the course of the eight paragraphs, the writer has regulated the direction of the line of reasoning by signaling three changes. Each signal differs from the others in type and length, but they all perform the same function. The writer is not yet done with an "assessment of the situation"; the line of reasoning to this point implies that a conclusion will follow, and you can probably foresee how it will develop. In Chapter 14, we will present that conclusion as an illustration of the strategy of concluding. We have thus far illustrated how a writer monitors the flow of information in the body of a statement.

Summary

To build an expanding sequence into a coherent line of reasoning, one strategy is to monitor the sequence—to be aware of changes from one category of information to another and to signal those changes for the reader. The signal shows how the assertions in any category of information relate to your tentative organizing idea. Your signal can be an assertion, a string of assertions, a paragraph—whatever is needed to make the change of direction explicit.

Applying the Concept: Monitoring an Extended Statement

Chapter 12 has shown how monitoring an extended statement helps to establish its coherence. Experienced writers and editors ensure such coherence by using various strategies. Studying these strategies and employing some of them will give you the same advantage in your own writing.

Professional writers or editors often indicate categories by way of headings within a developing line of reasoning. These headings label the next category of information. Find some magazines—such as *Atlantic Monthly, Fortune, Harper's, New York, Psychology Today, Science,* or *Scientific American*—which have used this strategy. Then try to decide whether the writer or editor has effectively indicated shifts in the line of reasoning. For example, would you remove some headings, thereby making larger categories, or would you subdivide some categories into smaller units? If these headings were removed, would you be able to see how each new category of information relates to the developing organizing idea and to previously mentioned categories? In those cases in which the extended statement would not be coherent if headings were removed, could you re-establish coherence by making the relationships among categories more explicit? If so, how?

Next look at essays that do not include headings. Try to infer the categories the writer has established. Are shifts between categories clearly indicated—even without headings? If not, how might the writer have more effectively monitored the extended statement? You might want to review the writer's organizing idea in order to build the assertions into a line of reasoning that explicitly establishes relationships among its parts.

Probably the most useful way to study the concept of monitoring an extended statement is to analyze one of your earlier essays or one that you are currently writing by asking appropriate questions. You and your classmates might discuss strategies for monitoring by sharing papers and suggesting revisions for one another, in which case the following questions will be useful:

1. How clearly does each category in the extended statement follow from those that precede it, and how clearly does it lead to those that follow it?
2. Has the writer clearly and adequately monitored the shift from one category to another?
3. Is the pattern of relationships among the categories in the extended statement self-evident?

13. Using Strategic Repetition

In Chapter 12, we stated that writing is coherent when the logic of its sequence of assertions is self-evident. You achieve the desired coherence by relating each assertion in your line of reasoning to the other assertions around it and also to your developing organizing idea. When you first forecast the direction of a statement, you begin the process of creating sequential logic. But this forecast alone is not sufficient to guarantee coherence; it will not fully satisfy the reader's need to recognize the connections maintained through each successive paragraph. So you continue to signal what you will write, relating it to what you have already written, until a conclusion is in view.

One important way to sustain the coherence of a statement is to recall aspects of your forecast periodically as the line of reasoning evolves. Specifically, you recall the forecast at those points in your writing where one category of information is about to lead to another. You show the reader how this new information relates to what has come before and also what you think its significance will be to the fully developed statement.

But there is also a second means of sustaining coherence. As you write, you can reveal the network of relationships in a system of assertions by a process of **strategic repetition;** that is, you can use repetition to reveal how each assertion connects to the one preceding and anticipates others to follow. By recalling the forecast, you show your reader the broad structure of a statement, and by using strategic repetition, you show the specific association between any two assertions. When you coordinate the two means of sustaining coherence, you make your writing clear to your reader, and you also expand it to its full potential.

What Is Strategic Repetition?

Engineers often speak of repetition as *redundancy*. The Apollo moon rockets, for example, included redundant systems as a safeguard against breakdowns. For every important system in these rockets, a back-up was installed to do exactly the same job if the primary system failed. These systems were redundant, therefore, because they performed the same task.

Redundancy is also a natural feature of language. In spoken language, if one sound fails to convey its signal, other sounds will back it up. If one word fails to convey a significance, the sentence pattern provides other words to reinforce it. Such redundancy enables a listener to understand a message without hearing it perfectly, as in the case of a bad telephone connection.

Because redundancy is a natural characteristic of language, you can make it work for you in your writing. You can use it to control the development of a tentative organizing idea. Unlike speaking, however, writing requires deliberate and strategic repetition: you intentionally repeat important pieces of information at critical points in a statement. This repetition serves both as a reminder and as a forecast. It creates emphasis by restating information, and it shows the reader how what comes next follows reasonably from what has gone before. Strategic repetition shows the reader how the writer intends assertions to be interrelated; therefore, it holds an extended statement together for the reader.

Repetition is ineffective when there is too much or too little of it. If it is too literal, it merely calls attention to itself. On the other hand, if it is too fragmentary, it causes confusion about how the assertions of a statement relate to one another. Useful repetition, however, depends on the writer's skill in linking assertions. It makes connections explicit in order to reveal the logical progress of the statement. And it does so without attracting the reader's notice.

The Kinds of Strategic Repetition

There are two types of strategic repetition, grammatical and logical. *Grammatical repetition,* which is simpler, is achieved by sentence overlap. It operates on the surface of a statement explicitly to relate one sentence to another, and thereby reduces verbal ambiguities. Consider this example:

The dragon ate its mother.
Then, having dined, it retired to its den.

The second sentence overlaps the first in several ways. "Having dined" repeats the verb in the first sentence, though in a different form. The subject of the first sentence, "the dragon," is twice repeated by the two pronouns of the second sentence, "it" and "its." The new information in the second sentence is that the dragon retired to its den. But the writer provides this new information in the context of the earlier information to show how the dragon's second action is related to the first.

Logical repetition, the second type, occurs in the structure of a statement. It is subtler and more important than sentence overlap because it reveals the logic of a line of reasoning rather than the mere relationship of sentences. Just as sentence overlap is a way of reducing verbal ambiguities, so overlap among the assertions is a way of reducing logical ambiguities. You deliberately repeat concepts that are common to more than one assertion in order to reveal the logical connections among the assertions. Specifying these connections helps you to expand and develop a statement to its logical completeness. By revealing your line of reasoning, you expand your own awareness of your subject.

Here is a simple example of logical repetition. Suppose the following two assertions appeared next to each other in a statement:

Human beings are rational.
Therefore, Socrates is rational.

Does the line of reasoning make sense? Yes, but only if you infer a missing assertion, namely, that Socrates is a human being rather than some other kind of creature. The argument can be stated more fully this way:

Human beings are rational.
Socrates is a human being.
Therefore, Socrates is rational.

In such a simple line of reasoning, there is no serious uncertainty even when the middle assertion is missing: the reader can easily make the leap (which involves a logical inference) from the first assertion to the last. But in less rigorous reasoning, a missing assertion can often cause serious confusion. The reader cannot make the connection between what has come before and what follows and will not see the logical continuity that the argument intends to establish.

To include the middle assertion in the line of reasoning above (that Socrates is a human being) is to provide strategic repetition. Here is why: the middle assertion repeats some of the information that was found in the first one; that is, both make reference to "human being." The second assertion relates Socrates to the subject of the first assertion. If Socrates is a species of "human being," and if a "human being" is rational, then Socrates must be rational—which is the conclusion of the chain of reasoning. The redundant second assertion is not vital to the argument's development because you can safely infer it, but including it gives the reader greater assurance about the writer's logic in moving from the first assertion to the third.

Here is another example, where the repetition plays a more important role in the development of a line of reasoning. Assume that the following assertions have been abstracted from a statement and that each assertion represents a paragraph:

1. Children are not born as Democrats or Republicans.
2. A person's parents often determine that person's political bias.

Does the second assertion logically follow from the first? No indeed. It happens to follow in sequence, but it does not logically follow. The second assertion is not yet a consequence of the first. (You can test the logic of any concluding assertion by placing the word *therefore* in front of it to see if it actually follows from the preceding assertions.) In this case, there is a gap between these two assertions. Can you see that at least one other assertion (and perhaps more) must occur between them in order to relate them?

Suppose you choose the following assertion to relate these other two:

1a. Children are influenced in their political choices before they are old enough to vote.

Does this assertion establish a logical relationship? Not yet. It is a good start, but only a start. With this assertion you have a possible reason for the fact that children who are not born as Democrats or Republicans grow up to become one or the other. That is to say, you have one possible way of linking the two assertions you began with. But there are potentially dozens of reasons for the political consciousness of the maturing individual. What makes parental influence all that special? How is the reader to progress from the fact that people join political parties to the supposition that parental influence is the most important reason? The leap is simply too far.

Even with this new assertion (that children are subject to influence), it is difficult to see what relationships the writer intended, because there is not yet enough logical overlap in the information. But the writer can strengthen the argument by expanding it and by incorporating a greater degree of repetition. The writer can shorten the logical leaps by making more assertions, for example:

1b. Most children grow up under the supervision of their parents.
1c. Attitudes of children often resemble those of their parents.
1d. Children tend to be influenced politically as well as in other ways by their parents.

Given these assertions, it is possible to conclude, "Therefore, a person's parents can determine his or her choice of party." This at least would be an arguable case for the importance of parental influence on the development of political consciousness, whether or not a reader agrees with it. More to the point, the writer has revealed a coherent line of reasoning by shortening the leaps from one assertion to the next.

This set of assertions could be organized in several ways. Here is one way:

1. Children are not born as Democrats or Republicans.
    1a. Children are influenced in their political choices before they are old enough to vote.
        1b. Most children grow up under the supervision of their parents.
        1c. Attitudes of children often resemble those of their parents.
        1d. Children tend to be influenced politically as well as in other ways by their parents.
2. Therefore, a person's parents often determine that person's political bias.

Notice the amount of repetition in all the assertions. For example, 1b, 1c, and 1d are related by the fact that parents are in a unique position to influence the behavior of their children. There is also new information in each assertion:

(1b) children are supervised by their parents
(1c) children are apt to have the same attitudes as their parents

(1d) children can be politically influenced by their parents

But the new information is conveyed in each case by means of a logical overlap with information that the reader has already received. At every point in the developing reasoning, you can see how what has gone before relates to, and anticipates, what is to come next. This repetition enables you to see at the same time how the writer's thought is evolving.

If you were to expand each of these assertions into a new paragraph, you would expand the entire statement from the original two paragraphs to a new total of six. It is not the increase in words, however, that makes a statement complete. Rather, it is the chain of assertions— with no logical gaps—that completes it. Strategic repetition, both grammatical and logical, enables you to say everything you want to say. You expand a statement by repeating words and concepts that have occurred in previous assertions. A concept worth repeating may have been stated explicitly or implied, but in any case you perceive it as being common to more than one assertion. By this means you specify a reasoning process and thereby complete your statement.

Strategic Repetition: An Illustration

The line of reasoning that follows is missing a possible middle assertion. Given the two assertions, A and C, see if you can furnish a third assertion, B, that will relate A to C through repetition. Then notice how each assertion can be expanded into a paragraph in order to develop a complete written statement.

ASSERTION A

The enforcement of laws is essential to social order and to the protection of our civil rights.

ASSERTION B

(Think of a possible middle assertion.)

ASSERTION C

Police forces, therefore, are essential to social order and to the protection of our civil rights.

In order to derive assertion B, you must assess the implications of the two assertions you began with. What have they in common? How can you move logically from A to C? You do it by making explicit the implications you see in the association of A and C. If the writer is arguing that police forces are essential, then he or she must be implying the fact that police forces are agencies of law enforcement—and probably the most effective agencies. Hence:

ASSERTION B
Police forces are the most effective agencies of law enforcement.

EXPANSION OF THE ASSERTIONS INTO FULL PARAGRAPHS

ASSERTION A
Few would disagree that obedience to civil authority is essential both to the orderly running of a society and to the protection of its citizens. Most of us are also aware that some individuals willfully choose not to obey civil authority and in so doing, endanger the lives and rights of others. Without the law, and without some effective means of enforcing the law, antisocial individuals would be free to violate the rights of other citizens without fear of punishment. Law enforcement, therefore, is a vital element of society insofar as it prevents and penalizes violations of the civil order.

ASSERTION B
The most effective means of civil law enforcement is the police force, which is responsible for preserving the social order and for safeguarding the rights of citizens. Other types of law enforcement—ranging from individual retaliation ("an eye for an eye") to vigilante justice—have failed to promote "the greatest good for the greatest number." In these forms of enforcement, punishment is arbitrary and not subject to any form of legal control. In addition, the enforcement is not fair in its application and is motivated by self-interest rather than the interest of society as a whole. Only the well-trained police force, always subject to public control, can provide effective law enforcement.

ASSERTION C
It is clear, therefore, in spite of the popular arguments to the contrary, that police forces are vital to the preservation of social order and to the protection of the rights of individuals. Certainly, there have been abuses of police power, and certainly the bad police officer poses as serious a threat to our civil rights as any criminal. But abuses only suggest the importance of defining and restricting the powers and responsibilities of any police force so that such a force truly answers to the society it is designed to serve. Arguments for

abolishing police agencies fail to consider the social realities and human failings that have made necessary the very institution of law. If we need law, and if we have found no more efficient an agency for its enforcement than the civil police, then evidently we must continue to maintain our police forces as the best safeguard of our social order.

Summary

A writer cannot assume that a forecast will satisfy the reader's need to recognize the sequential logic of a statement. It is necessary to continue to monitor throughout the length of your statement. By continuing to monitor, you reveal to your reader some relationship between what you have already said and what you are likely to say as you continue writing.

You can reveal the network of relationships in any system of assertions by the process of strategic repetition. There are two kinds of strategic repetition: grammatical repetition, which explicitly relates one sentence to another, and logical repetition, which reveals implicit connections between assertions in a line of reasoning. As you clarify the connections you are making by the process of strategic repetition, you expand your own—and your reader's—awareness of your subject.

Applying the Concept: Strategic Repetition

When a statement fails to convince its intended reader, the cause is often the reader's inability to grasp connections that the writer intends to make but has not made explicit. Logical gaps between the writer's assertions create uncertainty in readers about the precise relationships they are meant to perceive. You can make your writing both clearer and more convincing by closing such unintentional gaps wherever you find them.

Read the first draft of a statement you have begun to write, or better yet, ask other readers, perhaps your classmates, to do so. Can you or these other readers detect logical gaps between any two of its assertions? You can test for such gaps by asking if there is a clear and evident connection between the assertion you are now reading and the one just before it. Whenever you suspect that the answer may be no, copy on a separate sheet of paper the two assertions that appear to be ambiguously or incompletely related; put one at the top of the sheet and the other at the bottom.

Now see how many intermediate assertions you can find that will help link the two you started with and list them on your sheet. Ask your classmates to follow the same procedure; you may be surprised at the differences between their new connecting assertions and your own. Add to your list any of your classmates' assertions that you think are useful to your line of reasoning.

Then rewrite the part of your statement that contains the two initial assertions, including the newly expanded segment of your line of reasoning. Notice that your statement is now both longer and more explicit than before. Continue to look for other logical gaps in your reasoning and repeat this process of expansion whenever you find them. Remember that the effectiveness of a statement depends on a reader's ability to discern connections among its assertions. The easier you make the reader's process of discovery, the more convincing your writing will be.

You can also practice using strategic repetition in class by making up any two assertions and then trying, either individually or in groups, to find several additional assertions that can be placed in a sequence between them so as to make their connection explicit. You might start, for instance, with these two assertions:

A. Noise levels in centers of dense population have reached intolerable proportions.
B. We must alter the approach patterns of commercial jets.

Can you create a sequence of intermediate assertions that will link A to B? Or try this pair:

A. Workers in foreign countries are often more industrious than workers in our own.
B. Our government should restrict the quantity of foreign merchandise coming into the United States.

This procedure of building overlapping assertions will help develop your ability to make tighter connections. You may want to use the following questions to assess your effectiveness in making logically explicit connections when you are writing.

1. Does the writing contain some repetition of its early assertions?
2. Is strategic repetition used to reveal the network of relationships that comprise the statement?
3. Is the strategic repetition used as a reminder? Does it reformulate earlier assertions?
4. Is strategic repetition used as a forecast? Does it show the reader how what comes next follows reasonably from what has gone before?

14. Developing a Conclusion

In Parts 3 and 4, we described a written statement as a sequence of related assertions that progresses toward some destination. We also explained how to make your reasoning apparent to an intended reader through initial forecasting, monitoring, and strategic repetition. In Chapter 14, we will describe the last phase of writing, which is the inferring of a conclusion that represents the writer's fully developed organizing idea.

Not all writing proceeds to a developed conclusion. Chapter 10 introduced the diminishing sequence as a model of writing that begins with a main idea adequate to the writer's purpose and then merely elaborates or clarifies it through successive paragraphs. In that model, the writer's personal learning is subordinated to the needs of intended readers: efficient communication takes precedence over the writer's thorough exploration of the subject. What follows the main idea may specify the writer's information and insights, but it does not ordinarily extend them.

However, in Chapter 11, we described a more flexible model that encourages the writer's learning at the same time as it takes into account the reader's implied questions. Writing that evolves as a controlled expanding sequence of assertions can be especially rewarding because the knowledge you end up with is often much richer than the tentative insights with which you began. Essay writing typically follows the model of a controlled expanding sequence, for instance, newspaper editorials, articles in feature magazines, or the essays you compose in your history, literature, or political science courses. Reaching conclusions in these kinds of writing can be an adventure: you discover what you meant to say through the process of attempting to say it. This chapter is concerned with reaching a conclusion as the natural culmination of any controlled expanding sequence of assertions.

What Is a Conclusion?

A **conclusion** is an inference, a decision you make about the significance of interrelated assertions. You cannot make this decision when you start to write a statement. It becomes increasingly possible only as you write.

In Chapter 9, we defined a written statement as a system of connected assertions. The conclusion of a statement is an assertion that completes your reasoning. It reflects a developed understanding of the implications of a line of thinking. It is partly an insight and partly a decision that something reasonably follows from whatever has gone before. It is the writer's most developed judgment about the significance of the whole system of assertions.

What are the features of a conclusion? The question can easily be answered with reference to the strictest kind of argument, the syllogism from classical logic. Most lines of reasoning are not as limiting as the syllogism, and very few written statements elaborate that kind of argument. Nevertheless, the syllogism provides a simple example.

One form of the syllogism looks like this:

$$A \text{ is } B$$
$$C \text{ is } A$$
$$C \text{ is } B$$

The first two equations in this model are premises; the third equation is a conclusion. The function of the first two equations is to predict the third. Here is an example of a syllogism, one which you will recall from Chapter 13.

> Human beings are rational.
> Socrates is a human being.
> Therefore, Socrates is rational.

Notice two interesting facts about the conclusion of this argument. (1) All the information in the conclusion can be found in the premises, but not in the same relationship that the conclusion establishes. The premises furnish the information from which the conclusion will be derived; they imply the conclusion. (2) Moreover, the conclusion is a new assertion that is not precisely stated at any earlier stage of the argument. That Socrates is rational is the writer's own discovery about the significance of the information as it develops from the premises of the argument. The rationality of Socrates is what the writer has come to understand from the implications of this line of reasoning.

The developed conclusion of any statement is not contained in the premises but in the interrelationships among them. A conclusion follows from a system of assertions, but it also extends the significance of that system in some way.

A conclusion is derived from the line of reasoning that precedes it, but it is also a new assertion, a new kind of information that the writer recognizes only by writing. The conclusion is a discovery as well as a summary. This newly discovered assertion may resemble the tentative organizing idea at the beginning of the writer's statement, but it has also progressed and expanded beyond that tentative idea by means of the implications in an evolving line of reasoning.

The conclusion of any statement possesses these characteristics whether or not it is a syllogism. A syllogism is an argument that arrives at a necessary conclusion using no more than two previous assertions. Most lines of reasoning are not this limiting. Any number of assertions may constitute a statement, sometimes many more than the syllogism possesses. Moreover, a number of different conclusions might be possible for a given statement, depending on the interrelationships among assertions along the way. Any evolving line of reasoning restricts the writer to certain kinds of conclusions but not to any one conclusion.

Regardless of the type of statement, the conclusion is derived from the chain of assertions that precede it, yet is different from any one of the assertions that give rise to it. A conclusion is a discovery as well as a summary. Given an assertion A, followed by B, followed by C, followed by D, the developed conclusion represents a gradual recognition that some new assertion X is the one the writer was looking for in the first place.

Recall the illustration from Chapter 12 regarding the crisis in urban education. Here is the way a conclusion to that statement can evolve through the implications of its line of reasoning.

The chain of assertions, you will remember, developed in this way:

TENTATIVE ORGANIZING IDEA

   The causes of inequities between urban and suburban schools must be considered before we can contemplate a solution.

SUBSEQUENT ASSERTIONS

1. Adequate facilities and qualified teachers are provided for children from wealthy homes but not for children from poor homes.
2. Shortcomings in urban schools have often been attributed to lack of funds.
3. Economists support this view.
4. The problem is not merely economic; it runs deep in the American system of values.
5. The schools are a middle-class instrument used to "Americanize" the children who attend them.
6. School boards are dominated by representatives of the middle class.
7. Inner-city children are alienated from the schools.
8. As institutions of the middle class, the schools do not adequately serve the needs of city children.

These assertions imply a range of possible conclusions, but before writing any conclusion, it will be helpful to retrace the writer's line of reasoning.

The writer's tentative organizing idea is his or her best estimate of how the statement is likely to develop. The writer knows that the conclusion will develop from the causes for the inequality of urban and suburban schools. But solutions to the problem that adequately address these causes are not yet clear.

The argument contains seven assertions. The first assertion (about unequal staff and facilities) simply states the case. The writer does not intend to prove this inequality but states a given situation in order to proceed to a discussion of its causes.

The second assertion (about the lack of funding) establishes the cause most commonly associated with the inequality, namely, the distribution of funds. Sensing that this cause is probably superficial, the writer states it early in order to clear away popular misconceptions before dealing with more subtle problems.

The third assertion (the economists' view) gives token support to the second assertion, which the writer will later disqualify.

The fourth assertion (that this is a problem of values) is the turning point in the statement. The writer is now going to analyze what appear to be the deeper causes of educational inequality.

The fifth assertion (schools are a middle-class instrument) equates the school system with a particular system of values. The writer is preparing to argue that this system of values, applied indiscriminately, penalizes urban students.

The sixth assertion (middle-class dominance of school boards) implies that all the schools serve middle-class interests.

The seventh assertion (the different needs of inner-city students) and the eighth assertion (urban schools do not serve these needs) explain why the schools have alienated inner-city children.

Now for the conclusion. What has really been the writer's purpose? Why elaborate the causes of educational inequality unless you are searching for a solution? The writer looks at the causes in order to come to some conclusion about changing the situation. You recall that a conclusion has two characteristics. It is implied in the line of reasoning that precedes it, yet it is a new assertion not specified at any earlier point in the argument.

What conclusion can the writer draw from the argument developed here? The writer cannot state a particular solution since the argument does not focus on the evaluation of solutions; instead, it stresses what any solution will involve. A simple cause of the problem, such as poor distribution of funds, could be easily removed by reallocating the funds. But the writer has found deeper causes—the biased values assumed by the schools and the resulting alienation of inner-city children. Such complex causes require a different order of response. Indeed, perhaps no response is possible; perhaps there is no immediately feasible solution, which is precisely the writer's developed conclusion. This conclusion is implied in the chain of reasoning, but it is not expressly stated in the assertions that anticipated it.

Here is a possible conclusion to this line of reasoning. (It happens to be a paragraph, but it could be a sentence, or two paragraphs, or the last chapter of a book: there is no set length to the conclusion of a statement.) Notice that it begins with a summary but ends with a new assertion. Read the last sentence first; then see how it derives from the assertions that precede it.

The problem we must confront, then, does not involve simply a redistribution of funds so that the urban schools can improve facilities, hire more staff, or provide better materials for students. The problem goes far deeper. It lies in our attitudes and expectations regarding what the public schools should be and what they ought to do. It concerns the role that schools should play in the development of children. To solve the problem, we must reappraise our traditional understanding of what the role might be. We must realize that different schools, with different populations of students, may need different kinds of support. *But unfortu-*

nately, because the problem is so intimately tied to a system of values that educational authorities take for granted, a workable solution may be a long time coming.

Now glance back at Chapter 12 and compare the opening paragraph of the statement on education with the concluding paragraph given here. Can you now see the difference between a forecasted tentative organizing idea and a developed organizing idea? Can you see how the second grows out of the first through the evolution of a system of assertions?

Developing a Conclusion: An Illustration

The system of assertions that follows exhibits a line of reasoning. See if you can recognize that line of reasoning, assess its implications, and then infer a conclusion that represents your estimate of the significance of the argument.

SYSTEM OF ASSERTIONS

TENTATIVE ORGANIZING IDEA

Forest fires destroy vast areas of timberland yearly, and since that land is the last escape we have from hectic city life, its loss can be measured in very human terms.

ASSERTIONS

Forest regions are among the last primitive areas available to most Americans living in crowded cities.

Access to forest regions allows for at least a brief escape from the frustrations of urban life.

Forest fires destroy thousands of acres of timberland each year.

Many fires are caused by freaks of nature such as lightning.

Many fires are also caused by human carelessness.

If we lose this last retreat from the crowded cities, we could end up forever trapped in them.

After scanning this system, can you think of a possible concluding assertion? Here is one such possibility, which follows from the system but also extends its significance:

We must make every effort to preserve our wilderness from the destruction brought by forest fires; in particular we must eliminate fires that are the result of human carelessness.

In an actual written statement, this conclusion could be a single sentence or a paragraph or a chapter. Here is a paragraph, for instance, that expands the concluding assertion:

The solution is obvious. To continue to enjoy the last remaining wilderness areas available, we must protect those areas from the massive destruction brought about each year by forest fires. Certainly we should keep up the fire watches so essential to forest preservation during the dry months. More important, we must guard against the campers and vacationers who annually burn down thousands of acres through carelessness. We must protect our forests from their worst enemy—not the forces of nature but the thoughtlessness of humans. When we endanger our wilderness retreats, we are endangering one of the last alternatives to the relentless pressures of urban life.

Summary

As you write, you refine and develop your tentative organizing idea through an expanding system of assertions. Gradually, you recognize that the implications of your system lead to a new assertion expressing the developed significance you have been looking for. This new assertion is the basis of your conclusion, which is both a summary of the writing that precedes it and also a statement of some new relationship following from your line of reasoning. In other words, the conclusion grows out of your system of assertions, but it also extends the reasoning to a final judgment about the value of what you are saying.

Applying the Concept: The Conclusion

Assessing the implications of a developing line of reasoning, whether it is your own or someone else's, requires concentration and practice.

The analytical skill involved is similar to that needed for math problems requiring you to predict the next number in a sequence based on the relationships between preceding numbers. An easy numerical sequence to assess is the following: 2, 4, 6, 8, 10, X. You know that the value of X is 12 because you have perceived an interval of $+2$ in the sequence up to that point. But here is a more difficult sequence: 40, 57, 72, 85, 96, 105, X. Can you see why X must equal 112? What number must follow 112 in this sequence? When you solve for the value of X in such puzzles, you discover the internal logic of the sequence of numbers that includes X. Your solution represents a conclusion about the relationship that makes the system of numbers coherent.

Deriving a conclusion for some verbal line of reasoning is usually a less precise activity than analyzing the intervals in a sequence of numbers. But the process of inference that enables you to arrive at a conclusion is similar. Consider a highly restricted verbal argument like the following:

A. A free society should afford women the same privileges as men.
B. The United States considers itself a free society.

What is the necessary conclusion of this sequence of assertions? You determine the conclusion by assessing the connections between the two assertions leading to it. Sentence A is more general than sentence B but is related to it through a common reference to "free society." The United States is a free society (B); *any* free society should support equal rights (A). Therefore, the United States should support equal rights— a conclusion that the relationship between the two assertions makes inevitable.

By analyzing still longer and less restricted arguments to determine plausible conclusions, you can strengthen your capacity to make similar assessments in your own writing. Consider the following sequence of assertions, for example. Can you suggest a conclusion suited to it? Remember that a conclusion both summarizes the argument preceding it and offers a new assertion that states some principal implication of that argument.

TENTATIVE ORGANIZING IDEA

Although science courses differ from humanities courses in subject matter, method, and purpose, each type has its own value in an educational program.

ASSERTION

The purpose of education is to multiply perspectives, to expand awareness, to develop the confident humility that results from a flexible outlook and a broad range of interests.

ASSERTION

The natural sciences extend our awareness of the physical world around us.

ASSERTION

Practical applications of the natural sciences can improve our relation to our environment and the quality of our lives.

ASSERTION

Courses in the natural sciences develop both technical skills and a self-disciplined, logical approach to the discovery of knowledge.

ASSERTION

The humanities—philosophy, literature, history, and the rest—are concerned with our peculiarly human needs, fears, and aspirations— and our ways of expressing them.

ASSERTION

Knowledge gained from the humanities can improve the quality of our relations with one another as mutually dependent members of the human family.

ASSERTION

Courses in the humanities develop our awareness of the spiritual, moral, and aesthetic values that make human life worthwhile and that distinguish it fundamentally from all other forms of life.

Your conclusion to this line of reasoning should follow from it but also extend its significance.

Here is an even more complex line of reasoning. Can you infer a plausible conclusion?

TENTATIVE ORGANIZING IDEA

The free expression of ideas is essential to any healthy society.

ASSERTION

New ideas are disconcerting; they challenge our preconceptions and threaten our settled and comfortable view of the world.

ASSERTION

Galileo shook the very foundations of theology when he questioned the Ptolemaic universe, in which the sun circled the earth and the earth was the center of the universe.

ASSERTION

There is no question that new ideas can be dangerous to the smooth and orderly running of a state or social institution.

ASSERTION

Thomas Paine and others throughout history have stirred social unrest and shown the way to bloody civil revolt.

ASSERTION

Social progress is almost always painful since it is achieved through the overthrow of earlier attitudes, beliefs, and social institutions.

ASSERTION

Progress is achieved only through the confrontation of the old and outworn with the new and revitalizing.

ASSERTION

The freedom to dissent from established ideas and institutions is necessary for progress.

ASSERTION

Suppression of dissent leads to social stagnation and eventual decay.

You and your classmates can practice inferring conclusions from your reading as well. Suppose, for example, that you select an essay or a short story from your composition reader. As you read the statement, pay attention to its evolving sequence of assertions. When you reach a point where you feel confident that you can estimate some plausible conclusion, stop reading. Now see if you can write an ending to the statement that represents your sense of the direction of its line of reasoning. Compare your ending to those of other students who have read the same statement and written their own conclusions. Compare it also to the actual ending of the essay or story. Can you account for the differences between your proposed ending and that of the original writer? Which seems more plausible? Is one more surprising or more interesting than the other? If so, why?

Finally, pay closer attention to the conclusions you write for your own statements. One way of working out the implications in an essay you are writing is to reduce it to its essential line of reasoning. You can do this by writing down an assertion that summarizes each of its paragraphs—in other words, the organizing idea of each paragraph—and then arranging those assertions in a sequence representing your line of reasoning. Then, evaluate the logic of the sequence as you have done in the exercises above and infer a concluding assertion. You can then use that assertion to conclude your statement, either as a single sentence or a paragraph or even several paragraphs.

For analyzing conclusions already written and for making your own, you will find these questions to be useful guidelines.

1. Does the conclusion evolve from the major assertions that precede it?
2. Does the conclusion readily follow the last given assertion?
3. Does the conclusion represent a new discovery about your line of reasoning, or does it merely summarize earlier assertions?

Review of Part 4

The concepts discussed in Part 4 were monitoring an extended statement, using strategic repetition, and developing a conclusion. The descriptions of these concepts included procedures for ensuring the coherence of your statement even as you are writing it. Coherence, you recall, is what a line of reasoning possesses when the logic of its sequence of assertions is self-evident. Writing is coherent to the degree that it reveals the interrelationships among its assertions.

The Essential Concepts of Part 4

You can **monitor a line of reasoning** by focusing your attention on each shift from one category of information to another and by signaling that shift, whenever appropriate, to a reader. Your signals reinforce the coherence of your statement by revealing the relationship between each category and your tentative organizing idea. Once you yourself understand that relationship, you describe it while moving from one category to the next in order to make your line of reasoning explicitly clear. Employing such a strategy helps you to adhere to a line of reasoning as well as to reveal its logic to your reader.

You can make use of **strategic repetition** to reveal to your reader the relationships in any system of assertions. One form of repetition is *grammatical*—the recurrence of key words or similar words or the same syntactic patterns from one sentence to the next. Used sparingly, this verbal overlap can minimize ambiguities. A more effective strategy is *logical* repetition, which occurs within the reasoning of a statement by providing overlaps among the relationships that are expressed in successive assertions. In this case, the repetitions are conceptual rather than merely verbal.

Strategic repetition is an intentional and controlled echoing of important relationships at critical points in a statement. Such repetition establishes the coherence of your writing in two ways:

1. It reinforces important information to help the reader remember what the writer considers most significant.
2. It shows the reader how successive assertions interrelate by clarifying what the assertions have in common and by revealing how one follows plausibly from another.

Strategic repetition, therefore, makes the reader conscious of the sequential logic of a writer's statement by making explicit the logical connections among its assertions.

A **conclusion** can reinforce the coherence of your statement. Note, however, that a conclusion is more appropriate to an expanding sequence than to a diminishing sequence, in which the most important assertions appear first. Writers typically end a diminishing sequence by completing the final category of information with little or no summary of what has gone before. No assertion at the end of such a sequence extends the reasoning beyond the limits predicted at the start.

An expanding sequence, on the other hand, encourages you to perceive more about your tentative organizing idea simply by writing about it, so a controlled expanding sequence needs a conclusion. To represent your full understanding, the conclusion should be more than merely a summary; it represents partly your insight and partly your decision that something reasonably follows from what has gone before. The conclusion presents some new assertion that was implied in the argument but not specifically stated in any earlier assertion; it logically follows from the system of assertions but also extends the significance of that system in some way. Thus, your conclusion presents a discovery as well as a summary.

Applying the Concepts of This Book

This book has focused on writing as a process, presenting concepts that enable any writer to achieve control of this process. Now that you have completed the book, you may find it useful to assess your ability to use

the various controls we have described. Choose any extended statement that you have already written, either one that you have completed or an early draft that you will rewrite later. Once you have chosen a piece of writing, analyze its components, using the following sets
of questions. These questions can help you discover which parts of
your statement are still incomplete and in need of some revision.

Look first at the forecast of your writing and ask yourself these
questions:

1. Does it focus on a reader, acknowledging the reader's frame of
   reference?
2. Does it express a tentative organizing idea?
3. Does it indicate categories of information relevant to the organizing
   idea?
4. Does it suggest a sequence to those categories?
5. If your answer is no to any of these questions, how would you revise
   your forecast?

Next, look at the paragraphs that follow your forecast. The assertions in each paragraph should convey a unified significance that is
either explicit or implicit. You can ask yourself these questions about
each paragraph:

1. Does the paragraph convey an organizing idea explicitly? (Can you
   point it out?)
2. Can you write a sentence that summarizes the paragraph?
3. Is all the information relevant to the organizing idea of the
   paragraph?
4. Is the evidence sufficient to support the organizing idea?
5. If your answer is no to any of these questions concerning any paragraph, how might you revise that paragraph?

Now check the organizing ideas of successive paragraphs, inferring
them where they are not explicit. Do they form a *sequence* of assertions
and not merely a collection? These questions will help you to evaluate
whether or not your successive organizing ideas make a coherent
sequence.

1. Does the forecast convey an organizing idea for the entire statement?
2. Are the separate categories of information in the forecast clearly evident in the succession of organizing ideas for individual paragraphs?
3. Does the first paragraph following the forecast clearly relate to the
   forecast?

4. Is the organizing idea of each paragraph clearly related to the organizing idea of the preceding paragraph or else to a category of information in the forecast?
5. Have you included all the categories of information and all the major assertions you need in order to support the organizing idea of your statement?
6. If your answer is no to any of these questions, how might you revise your sequence?

Finally, look at your conclusion if you have written a controlled expanding sequence. Ideally, it will summarize your statement and also provide some new insight that your line of reasoning has made apparent. Asking these questions about your conclusion will help you assess it.

1. Does the conclusion summarize your system of assertions?
2. Does the conclusion assert some new insight that was implied in the system of assertions?
3. If your answer is no to either of these questions, how might you revise the conclusion?

You can use this check list of questions any time you write. In fact, unless you continue to ask these or similar questions about your future writing, you may not retain the control of choices that you have now achieved. It is easy to revert to old habits that may interfere with discovering an organizing idea and communicating it to an intended reader. But the questioning writer will remain alert to the demands of learning and communicating. Although you may still want to ask others for advice about revising your writing, you alone can decide the choices that will convey your purposes and meanings. You alone can build on what you have learned by being consciously critical about what you write.

Glossary

ASSERTION

An assertion is any sentence that establishes a relationship among pieces of information. An assertion conveys the significance of that information. (Chapter 1)

CATEGORIZING INFORMATION

To categorize your information is to infer some mutual connections among pieces of information and to state each of those connections in a word or short phrase. (Chapter 8)

COHERENCE

Coherence is a quality of relationship among the parts of any structure or system. An extended statement is a system of interrelated assertions about a subject, and it is coherent to the degree that it reveals the interrelationships among its assertions. In other words, an extended statement is coherent to the degree that its sequence is self-evident to the reader. (Chapter 12)

COMMON READER

The common reader is a model that you can construct in your mind when you do not know exactly who your reader is. You create this all-purpose reader on the basis of characteristics that all readers share, namely, their ignorance of your organizing idea and their impatience to find out the significance of your organizing idea. The common reader is about your age, has reached your level of education, and knows approximately as much about your subject as you do. (Chapter 6)

CONCLUSION

A conclusion is an inference, a decision you make about the significance of interrelated assertions. The developed conclusion of an extended statement is not contained in the premises but in the interrelationships among them. A conclusion follows from a system of
assertions, but it also extends the significance of that system in some
way. (Chapter 14)

CONTROLLED EXPANDING SEQUENCE

A controlled expanding sequence combines the advantages of both
the diminishing sequence and the expanding sequence. The controlled expanding sequence describes a progressive order of assertions wherein later assertions, broader and richer than those earlier,
represent the writer's growing understanding of the tentative organizing idea introduced at the start.

This combined reader-writer sequence allows you to explore your
subject as fully as you wish and to arrive at the full meaning of what
you want to say, doing so efficiently and satisfying the reader's
needs at the same time. (Chapter 11)

DIMINISHING SEQUENCE

A diminishing sequence is one possible order for the consecutive assertions in an extended statement. It is an order of descending
priorities. When you present information in a diminishing order of
importance, you are presenting a diminishing sequence. In a diminishing sequence, the writer's search for new meaning is subordinate
to a concern for efficient communication to the reader.

The most familiar example of the diminishing sequence is the
model that news writers follow, sometimes called the inverted pyramid. (Chapter 10)

EVIDENCE

Evidence is the specific information you choose to include in your
statement to support your organizing idea. All evidence is information, but not all information is evidence. Evidence is any information that helps to support, clarify, or develop the organizing idea of
a statement. (Chapter 4)

EXPANDING SEQUENCE

An expanding sequence is any written statement that represents a
growth in the development of your understanding; in such a sequence, later assertions are likely to be more important than earlier
ones because they reflect a clearer awareness of what you are trying

to say. By permitting new discoveries, the expanding sequence allows for a conclusion that is more significant than any assertion that has led up to it, a conclusion that represents a new awareness of the significance of your tentative organizing idea. The advantage of the expanding sequence is that it enables you to learn as you go. (Chapter 11)

EXTENDED STATEMENT

An extended statement is a system of assertions that support a tentative organizing idea, wherein each assertion depends on other assertions before it and anticipates those that follow it. In other words, an extended statement is a line of reasoning; it is a logical progression from one assertion to another that begins with a forecast of some sort and concludes when the writer's purpose is fulfilled. (Chapter 9)

FOCUSING ON A READER

To focus on a reader is to anticipate that reader's response by inferring what feelings, assumptions, experiences, or values will influence that reader's response to your subject. (Chapter 5)

FORECAST

A forecast is a preview of the writer's extended statement. Ideally, it presents three indicators of the forthcoming line of reasoning—first, a tentative organizing idea; second, the categories of information the writer expects to address; and third, a sense of the sequence in which those categories will be addressed. Forecasting is a means of orienting the reader, and it helps the writer to develop a precise line of reasoning. (Chapter 8)

FUNCTIONAL EVIDENCE

Functional evidence is the information that most clearly and persuasively conveys your organizing idea to your intended reader. It supports, clarifies, and develops your organizing idea in a way that enables that reader to comprehend it. (Chapter 7)

INFORMATION

Information consists of all those data that you might use in order to compose a written statement. The notes that you jot down about a subject are pieces of information. Such notes may be derived from your memory, but they may also be derived from other sources, such as interviews, lectures, dialogues, or readings. These notes may sometimes take the form of sentences, but more often they are simply fragments, that is, single words or word groups. As you write you continually relate pieces of information. (Chapter 1)

MONITORING AN EXTENDED STATEMENT

To monitor your extended statement is to test it as you proceed. To make a controlled expanding sequence of assertions into a coherent extended statement, one strategy is to monitor the sequence: to be aware of changes from one category of information to another and to signal those changes to the reader. The signal is an answer to the question, "How does what I have said relate to what I want to say?" Specifically, it shows how the assertions in any category of information relate to your tentative organizing idea. Your signal can be an assertion, a string of assertions, a paragraph—whatever is needed to make the change explicit. (Chapter 12)

ORGANIZING IDEA

An organizing idea is an assertion that unifies other assertions. The organizing idea of a paragraph is the one central assertion that organizes separate assertions into a paragraph. It can be stated explicitly in the writing, or it can be implied by the way in which individual assertions refer to some relationship they have in common. (Chapter 2)

Just as an organizing idea unifies assertions in a paragraph, it can also unify a series of paragraphs, that is, an extended statement. (Chapter 8)

PURPOSE

A purpose is simply a motive or reason for carrying out a task. The writer's purpose is whatever the writer wants to achieve by writing. You usually want some particular response from a reader, in which case you usually have some notion of what your purpose is. But you might also have several goals for any written statement, not all of which are clear to you when you begin. (Chapter 3)

READER'S FRAME OF REFERENCE

A reader's frame of reference is a composite of his or her feelings, assumptions, experiences, and values. It is that person's perspective or world view. (Chapter 5)

READER'S IMPLIED QUESTION

The reader's implied question represents the reader's attempt to relate your organizing idea to his or her own perspective or frame of reference. This implied question is essentially "What will this statement mean to me?" Any given written statement usually provokes some version of this question. (Chapter 6)

SEQUENCE OF CATEGORIES

The sequence of categories in any extended statement is determined by the order in which the writer names them in the forecast. You determine their order by deciding which sequence most effectively conveys your organizing idea to your intended reader. (Chapter 8)

STRATEGIC REPETITION

A second means of sustaining the coherence of an extended statement is to reveal the network of relationships in a system of assertions by a process of strategic repetition. That is, you can use repetition to reveal how each assertion connects to the one preceding and anticipates others to follow. You intentionally repeat important pieces of information at critical points in your statement.

This repetition serves both as a reminder and as a forecast. It creates emphasis by reformulating information, and it shows the reader how what comes next follows reasonably from what has gone before. Strategic repetition shows the reader how the writer intends assertions to be interrelated; therefore, it holds an extended statement together for the reader. (Chapter 13)

SUBJECT

A subject is whatever focuses your attention as you write. It is that part of your environment on which you are concentrating at any given moment. Your subject establishes the boundaries within which you search for information to include in your writing. (Chapter 1)

SYSTEM OF ASSERTIONS

Any written statement that reflects the writer's reasoned choices is a system of assertions. The statement may be merely a paragraph, or it may be more extended, composed of seven or eight—or more—paragraphs. (Chapter 9)

Index

Assertions
concept of, 52
continuity of, 25
defined, 12, 189
diminishing sequence of, 122–132
expanding sequence of, 133–144
and extended statement, 112–114
forecasting of, 115–119
leading to a conclusion, 174–183
making of, 12–14
nature of, 8–18
paragraph as a group of, 19
system of, 114, 174–183, 193
See also Extended statement

Categories, sequence of, 103–104
Categories of information, 103,
158–161, 189
Cause and effect, 10
Changes in direction, 156–161
Channeling, 115–118
Classification, 10
Coherence
defined, 154, 189
of an extended statement,
154–155
Coherence strategies, 154–187
conclusion development, 173–183
monitoring, 155–162
repetition, 163–172
summarized, 184–187
Common element, 16–17, 21
Common reader, 75–76, 89–90
Communication, between reader
and writer, 60–69
Communicative purposes, 32–36
Composing, writing as, 2
Conclusion, 173–183
defined, 174, 190
features of, 174–175
system of assertions for, 178–179
Continuity of assertions, 25
Controlled expanding sequence,
133–144

concept of, 146
defined, 137, 190
example of, 139–141
See also Expanding sequence

Developed conclusion, 173–183
assertion system for, 178–179
defined, 174
features of, 174–175
Diminishing sequence, 122–132
compared to expanding
sequence, 135–137
concept of, 146
construction of, 127–130
defined, 190
described, 123–127
news story as example of,
124–132

Evidence
concept of, 52
defined, 41, 190
as different from information,
41–42
functional, 81–88
nature of, 41–50
and organizing idea, 43–46
for the reader, 81–88
Expanding sequence, 133–144
compared to diminishing
sequence 134–137
concept of, 146
controlled, 133–144
defined, 135, 190–191
Expressive purposes, 32–36
Extended statement
coherence of, 154–155
coherence strategies for, 154–187
concept of, 114–115, 145
conclusion development, 173–183
construction of, 112–114
controlled expanding sequence
of, 133–144
defined, 112, 191
diminishing sequence of, 122–132

Houghton
Mifflin

ISBN: 0-395-31755-X

3-57505